THE OTHER OXFORD

THE OTHER OXFORD

The life and times
of Frank Gray and his father

CHARLES FENBY

Preface by Asa Briggs

LUND HUMPHRIES LONDON

© 1970 Charles Fenby

First edition 1970

Published by Lund Humphries Publishers Ltd
12 Bedford Square, London WC1

SBN 85331 278 8

Printed in Great Britain by
T. AND A. CONSTABLE LTD, EDINBURGH

In memory of F.G.

ACKNOWLEDGEMENTS

Frank Gray's papers were made available to me by the late William Sawyer of Jersey. In making use of them and for additional material, I have been greatly dependent on the publications owned by the Oxford Mail and Times Ltd., and would like to thank the Directors. I would also like to express my appreciation of the valuable assistance given by Walter Partridge in the preparation of the book and my thanks to Molly Duncan for her indefatigable patience.

C.F.

PREFACE

THERE have been many books about Oxford. Each new generation has added to the list, pointing to new pre-occupations and elucidating and reinterpreting past experience. Most of them, however, have concentrated upon the University, for long a world within a world, with its own traditions, customs and opinions. In the meantime, the city of Oxford has changed at least as much as the University, and particularly during the course of the last century, the transformation of the city has influenced the life of the members of the University to an unprecedented extent.

This new book, written on the basis of direct knowledge, tells a fascinating story of the other, neglected, Oxford. It is not only extremely interesting in its own right, but succeeds in illuminating many aspects of the changing relationship between city and university. Like many earlier books on Oxford it is rich in anecdote, crammed with living and often eccentric characters, sizzling with controversies. The university obviously had no monopoly of any of these, at least in the nineteenth and twentieth centuries.

Charles Fenby is admirably qualified to tell this story in which he himself is a character. He succeeds not only in chronicling episodes which will be unfamiliar to most of his readers but, what is far more difficult, in analysing human relationships and in recapturing mood and atmosphere. He takes us on a memorable journey into the past.

It is surely the right time for such a book to appear. Much of this history is not accessible in the form of documents; it relies on oral evidence which might otherwise be completely forgotten and draws upon insights into political procedures very different from those of our own society. There is a place for "principles", but what interests Mr Fenby most is the way in which principles were related to interests and the style in which they were expressed and promoted. The story starts in 1928, but it leads back into the heart of the nineteenth century and introduces personalities who left their mark on the city of Oxford even as it is today. Anyone who thinks he knows Oxford will learn much from this book.

Sussex, 1970.   ASA BRIGGS.

FOREWORD

THERE is a hallowed tradition about British public life according to which its conduct is pure and undefiled and never, well scarcely ever, deviates from the highest standards of integrity and probity. Of course, there have been occasional regrettable lapses but of such a trivial nature as not to affect the general pattern.

It may be dangerous to publish a story, or series of stories, which contradicts this soothing impression and which seems to show that behind the façade in comparatively recent times affairs were conducted by secret deals, family influence, jobbery and defiance of the law. Perhaps Oxford was unusual in its conduct. But perhaps it was most unusual in that some of the men who ran its affairs were were not hypocrites but gloried in candour. The danger is that the conventionally minded—and nobody likes to have an illusion weakened—may be shocked by the irregularities and give no credit for the honesty. In particular, Frank Gray, who provided much of the material in this book, may suffer as he did in his lifetime from the disapproval of the conventional who will react perhaps by thinking that he got no more than he deserved when he was driven out of public life.

The danger has to be ignored because he wanted everything to be known. Of course, most of his stories were told for a laugh (particularly at his own expense) but he was a true Liberal who believed that the people should not be hoodwinked. Whether everybody else in the story shared his honesty may be open to question.

CONTENTS

LIST OF ILLUSTRATIONS

INTRODUCTION

IN 1928, when I was 23 and had spent a couple of years in Fleet Street, I had the chance to go back to Oxford, this time not as an undergraduate but as a journalist. A new daily newspaper, the *Oxford Mail*, was planned and I was promised the editorship thanks to the fact that an uncle of mine was managing director of the group responsible for the enterprise.[1] Fortunately for me I was welcomed and indeed befriended by the local director, who had done a great deal to pave the way for the *Oxford Mail* and was to play the most important part at the most critical moment to make it a success. This was the famous Frank Gray, who had been at one time a spectacular figure in politics because he won two election campaigns of astonishing bitterness. He had maintained Oxford's reputation for political idiosyncrasy by getting himself unseated on petition, but he was still worshipped by the masses of Oxford city.

I first met Frank four years before, in the House of Commons, where as soon as we met he laughed and said, "He's studying my uniform". At Oxford, I had heard people say, "Anything but a black stock, my dear! That man, Gray, wears one." In the University at that time, he was thought of as a rabble rouser who spent his time flirting with women in the slums and bought their votes with free blankets (quite untrue). But what gave offence to stuffy people was his showman's appearance, in which the most important detail was a black stock tie, which he wore with a black coat and rather short sponge-bag trousers of a pronounced check. Out of doors he always wore slightly outsize grey Homburg hats and I afterwards discovered that he kept a big supply of these not only at home but at his office. He was a firm believer in the idea that a politician ought not to resort to anonymity but make himself recognisable.

[1] Sir Charles Starmer (1870-1933), founder of the Starmer Group of Newspapers, later to become the Westminster Press.

Apparently he was the chief shareholder in one of Oxford's two weekly newspapers, the Liberal *Oxford Chronicle*, which was remarkable for its University pages in which appeared the first published work of a number of undergraduates who were to become famous. But this sort of enlightenment brought no financial reward, rather the reverse, and it fell further and further behind its Conservative rival, the *Oxford Times*, which thrived on an unbroken diet of local news with no nonsense about culture. Frank tried to interest our newspaper group in his derelict weekly, but my uncle believed that with a population of nearly 100,000, Oxford could support a daily paper, so the *Oxford Chronicle* was closed down and the *Oxford Mail* started.

Into this venture Frank hurled all the energy which sooner or later—quite soon in this case—alienated his closest associates and, since he knew everybody in the city of Oxford and most of the people in the neighbouring counties, failure seemed out of the question. In course of time it became apparent that, while he was able to bring solid advantages to an enterprise of this sort, there were also disadvantages, for some of his more intimate personal relationships had developed into a state of extreme coolness; some of the local mandarins were willing to help us, but others—notable W. R. Morris,[1] the motor magnate, who had once been his closest friend—betrayed a deplorable prejudice. Frank's commonest boast was that he "bore malice to no man", which implied, of course, that in a great many cases he would have had every right to do so, but unhappily frailer mortals failed to extend a similar magnanimity to him and some were positively vindictive. However, that remained to be discovered and for the moment what mattered was his showmanship which encouraged both optimism and originality.

The symbol of this was the badge which he had manufactured for the newspaper's mast-head, a threefold display showing an unprecedented unity between not only the city and University of Oxford but also the rustic environs. The difficulty in completing this impressive trinity was that the county did not possess

[1] Later Viscount Nuffield (1877-1963). His family moved to Oxford from Worcester in 1880.

a coat of arms—at least none could be found—but Frank refused to be beaten and instructed the artist to use his imagination, with the result that when the *Oxford Mail* appeared it flourished an emblem, one part of which was invented for the occasion. Nowadays an appreciably different coat of arms for the county of Oxfordshire is publicly displayed, for instance by British Railways.

After designing this lucky charm Frank was concerned about getting the *Oxford Mail* published in time to make the claim which could never be gainsaid, that it was "Oxford's *First* Evening Paper". The reason for alarm was a rumour that our deadly rivals, the owners of the Conservative *Oxford Times*, were plotting to get in first with an evening paper before our machines were ready, but Frank hit on the idea of getting a few amateurish copies of the *Oxford Mail* run off every day for over a week so that they could be sent to the British Museum as evidence that, whatever our rivals claimed, ours was "Oxford's *First* Evening Paper".

As it turned out his prudence, though impressive enough at the time and doubtless infuriating to the owners of the other paper, eventually proved superfluous, for the *Oxford Evening Times* in making a first appearance had apparently overtaxed its strength and on some subsequent days failed to come out at all, so that when we appeared we had an even better slogan, "The daily that comes out *Every* day". What was more important, the other firm lost confidence and began to feel nervous about their weekly, which put them into the frame of mind to reconsider the attitude of proud local independence with which they originally received the intrusion of our newspaper group and weigh the secular advantages of reaching agreement.

It was a situation made for Frank. Some of the shareholders, and some of the staff on the *Oxford Times* might have been counted among his deadliest enemies, not merely because they had attacked him in print but because they had succeeded in driving him out of politics. But it gave him an opportunity to live up to his slogan of "bearing malice to no man" to such an extent that old political animosities evaporated in the atmosphere

3

of *bonhomie* which he created and any objection to the sale of the Tory paper to its old Liberal enemy was dismissed as mere bigotry. Thus the Newspaper Press of Oxford came together, if not in total amity at least in business partnership, and if any old-fashioned journalist was ill-advised enough to dwell on the more fanciful aspects of the operation he was quickly silenced by the realists who were anxious about their salaries.

Frank, at any rate, beamed more broadly than ever, and with justification for he had brought off a substantial *coup*, without which the *Oxford Mail* might well have gone under.

The newspaper office became the centre of his activities, the source from which his beam fell on the populace. Outside in the street there were usually a number of people waiting to see him to tell him their troubles or get a loan, and when I was with him I often had to produce half-crowns to give to the needy, for like many rich men he never had any cash on him but had to borrow when necessary. Not very tall, he walked with a heavy rolling gait which apparently became natural to him when he fought during the war as an infantry private. His face was florid with black hair combed back in a youthful style and he was always grinning. He loved to be called "puckish" or "impish" and the ambition to live up to these adjectives had become positively a vice. His grin was at its widest when inviting a laugh at his own expense, as when he once appeared at a solemn meeting wearing a resplendent fireman's uniform (he was an enthusiastic fire-fighter and was actually buried from a fire-engine). Because he encouraged an atmosphere of irreverence stuffy people thought him a clown, but he never seemed to mind. One of his favourite stories was about an election when a don at St John's was asked how he voted and said, "Frank Gray—but I held my nose when I did it". This offensiveness made me uncomfortable but Frank never seemed to mind. Perhaps he was expressing his opinion of dons.

During the first few months of the *Oxford Mail*'s existence I endured Oxford lodgings, but one day when I was at Frank's house he said, "Stay as long as you like, my boy" and so I moved in.

4

Shipton Manor, about seven miles from Oxford, is an outpost of the Cotswolds, a long low Manor House between the Banbury road and a canal. I remember it best in the atmosphere of high summer, when the chestnuts in the park were blown up as if about to sail into the sky and the canal was covered in a sickly green. The place was in a state of merciless activity, thronged with people who were all talking, arguing, quarrelling, playing games, driving cars, firing guns. Nobody was ever allowed a moment's rest. On one notable afternoon, a couple of ex-Presidents of the Oxford Union were striding up and down the drive in front of the house settling the world's affairs and apparently oblivious of half a dozen brass bands which were blowing their lungs out on the lawn in an annual competition.

There were so many guests for the week-end that a tent had been put up to accommodate a couple of young men. The others included a couple of dignified women whom Frank introduced to everybody as "two of the best gun-runners in the whole of Ireland". Everybody had to wake up in the morning at six o'clock because Frank fired an old shot-gun under the bedroom windows. He never went to bed before one and was always up at five or even earlier.

One wing of the house was given over to tramps, or tramp vagrants as Frank often called them, for he was devoted to the study of the men on the road. A year or two before he had turned himself into a tramp and toured the casual wards to expose the conditions there and now, although he had decided that the older men were beyond salvation, he still persevered with the job of trying to save the young. Anybody could get a bed here for a night but the men had to move on next day whereas the boys stayed on while Frank tried to get them to settle down. It was heart-breaking work and he used to say that he had only three successes: one a boy who made good in Canada, one a boy who took to the road because he was accused of stealing half a crown and afterwards won a college scholarship, and Billie. Frank was very proud of Billie because he found him out.

Apparently Billie said he had been brought up in a Poor Law school, never knew his parents, had worked on the land since leaving school and ran away from his last job. After he had been in the house for a fortnight Frank asked him whether he could ride and take big jumps, because it so he might be able to get a job with a cousin of Frank's who was an M.F.H. Billie was confident enough, which aroused everybody's suspicion for when has a farm labourer been able to ride? Moreover, he had a certain walk—and Frank had noticed a picture in the papers of the "Seventh Lancers embarking for Egypt". Billie was promptly accused of being a deserter and gave Frank enormous satisfaction by confessing without further ado. Instead of informing the police, Frank arranged for the boy to get the job but first addressed a lecture to him in the following terms: "It might save a lot of trouble if you would get out of that smart walk and do a bit of slouching about with your hands in your pockets."

The older men who used the tramps' wing were an anonymous lot, although there was a retired journalist who called occasionally with a bundle of cheques from 5s. upwards, had them cashed by Frank and then went off to get blind drunk. It was astonishing how we could live in the main part of the house, scarcely aware of the down-and-outs on the other side of the wall. I once passed a strange creature on the stairs who seemed dirty and dishevelled enough to be looking for the tramps' quarter but when I offered to show him the way he proved to be a well-known University man.

Frank was writing a book on tramps at the time, and most of the writing was done late at night when the guests had gone. He had a library looking out on the canal and the village church, whose parson was very much in disfavour for some obscure reason. Frank would stride about this study lighting cigarette after cigarette. I have never seen such a profligate smoker. Soon after lighting one cigarette he would put it down in an ash-tray and when he wanted to smoke again he would light another which in its turn would be put down, still burning, so that the room was permanently filled with smoke while he would sit at his desk in a corner stabbing at sheets of paper with a series of blunt pencils.

He was incapable of writing for long and periodically he would jump up, cough some of the smoke out of his lungs and stride to the fireplace against which he would lean with enormous satisfaction and say, for instance, "Well, here we are, my boy, aping the country gentleman!" The bigger the house-party the more raucously he derided the class we were "aping".

Visitors sometimes made the mistake of assuming that because their host was rich and successful he shared their conventional outlook on life. One evening, early in my stay, I got more and more indignant at dinner with a guest who went on and on about the iniquities of the working class, who did not want to work, wanted to live on the dole, etc., etc. It was a time of brutal unemployment. Afterwards in the library I began making an angry speech, which was cut short by a loud guffaw from Frank who said "Don't get excited, my boy. We're all working class here, but that fool didn't know it." He went on to recall a similar occasion in the past when an old housekeeper of his was helping at table and some guest talked in the same fashion as our guest that night. With intense glee Frank watched her turn pale with anger and seize a carving knife which, according to him, she would have plunged into the guest's back if he had not intervened. I never quite believed this story because I doubt whether he would have intervened.

Nothing suited him better than an outbreak of melodrama and what he found intolerably tedious was the interval between sensations. At this time, a married couple who could find nowhere else to live were allowed to put up a tent in the field near the main road and stayed there in ghastly squalor until one night a tremendous hubbub broke out and some of us rushed through the darkness to find one chasing the other (it was difficult to make out which) with a carving knife. Frank had great pleasure in separating them and somebody who knew him well said: "Well those people have justified themselves at last". He had great courage, and craved physical excitement. One evening, when he was bored, he challenged a friend to a motor-car race to Hyde Park Corner and led all the way until they were near the target when he thought he was going to be beaten and he rammed the other chap. They escaped with their lives.

7

The reason why he exploded sometimes was his fear of boredom and idleness which became something of a joke in the house. "Get pen to paper. Thought will follow", was the cry if anybody was caught deep in thought. It dated from the days when he was an articled clerk in London, and the oldest partner, a Mr Robinson, on being told by another clerk that he was "thinking about" a certain letter gave the reply: "Thinking about it! Thinking about it! Get pen to paper, *thought will follow.*" The cry suited Frank perfectly. He almost always knew at once what to do about a problem, but even when he was baffled he advocated action. "We're in a frightful mess, so all we can do is CONFUSE THE ISSUE"—this is what he advised on such occasions and we set about creating confusion.

He was a prolific story-teller and we encouraged him blatantly. At dinner an opportunity would inevitably come to tell one of his stories and one of us would open up the way by saying, "Now Frank", or "Now F.G." This was not a mere duty, but an admission that we enjoyed the stories however often we heard them. "Oo-ah" he would say in his Oxfordshire voice and the broadest grin would come on to his face and his eyes would glisten as he looked round the table, silently asking whether we who lived in the house could really bear hearing it again, but as far as I was concerned there was nothing I wanted more because at these moments his personality was radiant.

Most of these stories were about Oxford and the men who used to manipulate events in the convenient shadow of the well-known educational establishment, and many of them must have been handed down to him by his father who for over thirty years before the First World War had "ruled" this eccentric city. But what was notable about his own memories was the apparently limitless range of his personal relationships which was made possible by his classlessness and capacity to project the idea that he was merely "aping" the rich and successful. They embraced not only politicians, judges, lawyers, doctors, bankers and businessmen, but horse-dealers, gypsies, bookies, money-lenders, dog-breeders and scamps of all sorts. In fact, the man who appealed to him most was the man who lived by his wits, and if there was ever any question of impropriety in such a man's behaviour it was always discounted by the element of "courage and resource".

Listening to him in the dining-room at Shipton, with the candles burning and an occasional nondescript shuffling over the gravel outside to the tramps' quarters, it did at times seem as if Frank was a survival from a golden age when life was all excitement. But of course what he talked about usually was only the decoration of life, the illuminated spots and not a continuous story. Somebody ought to have written that story at the time, but nobody realised that the world Frank talked about and in which he once lived was already almost forgotten. He was the only witness and his too was a vanished supremacy.

In this attempt to tell the story I have left Frank himself to the second half. In the first I have described how his father Walter Gray came to Oxford, the sort of city he found and what he did to transform it.

WALTER GRAY AND THE LOCAL POWER STRUGGLE

PREFACE

THERE have been many books about Oxford. Each new generation has added to the list, pointing to new preoccupations and elucidating and reinterpreting past experience. Most of them, however, have concentrated upon the University, for long a world within a world, with its own traditions, customs and opinions. In the meantime, the city of Oxford has changed at least as much as the University, and particularly during the course of the last century, the transformation of the city has influenced the life of the members of the University to an unprecedented extent.

This new book, written on the basis of direct knowledge, tells a fascinating story of the other, neglected, Oxford. It is not only extremely interesting in its own right, but succeeds in illuminating many aspects of the changing relationship between city and university. Like many earlier books on Oxford it is rich in anecdote, crammed with living and often eccentric characters, sizzling with controversies. The university obviously had no monopoly of any of these, at least in the nineteenth and twentieth centuries.

Charles Fenby is admirably qualified to tell this story in which he himself is a character. He succeeds not only in chronicling episodes which will be unfamiliar to most of his readers but, what is far more difficult, in analysing human relationships and in recapturing mood and atmosphere. He takes us on a memorable journey into the past.

It is surely the right time for such a book to appear. Much of this history is not accessible in the form of documents; it relies on oral evidence which might otherwise be completely forgotten and draws upon insights into political procedures very different from those of our own society. There is a place for "principles", but what interests Mr Fenby most is the way in which principles were related to interests and the style in which they were expressed and promoted. The story starts in 1928, but it leads back into the heart of the nineteenth century and introduces personalities who left their mark on the city of Oxford even as it is today. Anyone who thinks he knows Oxford will learn much from this book.

SUSSEX, 1970.   ASA BRIGGS.

I

The Foundation
of Keble and North Oxford

FRANK'S father, Walter Gray, was born in 1848 as the result of a runaway match between a Cambridgeshire farmer's son and his sweetheart, who moved to Weston in Hertfordshire where the man, Thomas Gray, got a job as a hurdle-maker. He died in early middle age and left his widow with two sons but she was a woman of strong will and determination, and although she afterwards married again it was only when she could say she had brought up the family without anybody's help. Walter went to school at Stevenage and took his first job in a solicitor's office in Baldock. But the solicitor went bankrupt and the boy had to take a job with the Great Northern Railway, where the younger brother, William, spent all his life.

First Walter worked as a porter at Chalk Farm with two other men and there was only one bed in which all three slept on the shift system, but he used to say that he never slept better. He became a ticket-collector and then, when he was only 22, a stationmaster. This was at Waddington in Lincolnshire where he was his own clerk and ticket-collector, checked the goods traffic and made himself agreeable to the first-class passengers.

There was one important man who used Waddington station and this was a certain Colonel Shaw-Stewart who travelled a great deal to Oxford where he was involved in the plan to build a new college as a memorial to John Keble. This college was being founded, according to the preliminary announcement, with "the special object and intent of providing for persons desirous of academical education, and willing to live economically within a college wherein sober living and high culture may be combined with Christian training, based on the principles of the Church of England". But the governing body, to which Colonel Shaw-Stewart belonged, had a problem on its hands in appointing the first Warden, because although everybody agreed that the best man was the Rev. Edward Stuart Talbot, afterwards to be Bishop of Southwark and Bishop of Winchester, the difficulty was that Dr Talbot was married.

The moving spirit in the whole enterprise was Dr Pusey who said "I own that it was my ideal that the head of this college should live wholly amongst its members and, to speak plainly, a life of celibacy". But Dr Pusey was persuaded to change his mind. "When I heard," he said, "and knew whom he had chosen and who had chosen him, I felt that we had an additional gain—that one as chivalrous and devoted as himself would use that influence which is felt the more deeply because it can hardly be expressed in words—the influence over young and enthusiastic minds of a Christian lady."

What Dr Pusey may have found difficult to express in words was that Dr Talbot's bride was Lavinia, daughter of the fourth Lord Lyttelton, and therefore particularly influential. One of her brothers became a bishop, another a general, the third headmaster of Eton and the fourth a power at the Colonial Office. One of her sisters married Lord Frederick Cavendish, who was assassinated in Phoenix Park, Dublin; the other after outliving two fiancés, died before her contemplated marriage to A. J. Balfour. So the college founded for "humble students", who appreciated sober living and high culture, acquired no little social prestige.

However, the appointment did make it more difficult to organise economical living standards because a married Warden could hardly be expected to give all his time to the job, and what was needed was a Steward to look after the housekeeping. The founders hoped to make it possible for an undergraduate to

14

live at Keble for only £50 a year, including tuition fees, which meant there would have to be a great difference between life here and life in the older less economical colleges. For instance, he would have to breakfast in hall and never in his own room—an idea which hardly seemed feasible at the time and was jeered at many years later. The whole plan depended on getting servants of a quite different type from the older colleges. The Oxford "scout" had traditionally lived on perquisites made possible by rich or extravagant masters, who liked ordering turkey for breakfast, never inquired about mythical breakages and left the wine-bin to take care of itself. A new kind of staff had to be recruited and this meant a new kind of Steward.

Nobody knows why Colonel Shaw-Stewart thought his village stationmaster could do the job but he did. On his recommendation Walter went to Oxford, was interviewed, appointed and left Lincolnshire for Oxford where he had £50 a year and a free cottage.

Free from Oxford prejudices and ideas about "perquisites", Walter Gray got together an honest staff, kept it below the number suggested by the Governing Body and paid it slightly more than was paid in older colleges to compensate for the shortage of pickings. But where he was most successful was in his personal contacts, especially with the Talbot family. It was his outstanding stroke of luck that Dr Pusey had waived his objection to a married Warden, for Mrs Talbot's friends and relations liked Walter and A. J. Balfour, in particular, often dropped in for a chat about current affairs, valuable talk to a young man who was getting interested in the business world. Walter began reading the financial columns of the newspapers and talking about business to members of the Conservative Club which he joined, and he educated himself to such effect that he impressed Dr Talbot with his shrewdness. In fact, the Warden asked his advice about investing £100. When the advice was accepted and proved sound, his reputation as a financier was made and soon he was investing money regularly for a number of people, despising not even the washerwoman's mite.

One day Dr Talbot gave him some news. It was 1877 and a

15

Government Commission on the Universities was about to report. What Dr Talbot said was that this Commission would recommend that Fellows of Colleges should be allowed to marry. From time immemorial, only the heads of houses had been allowed to take wives, the other Fellows being condemned to Dr Pusey's celibate ideal, so Oxford at the time was almost entirely monastic, a conglomeration of colleges and small shops. But now houses would be needed, and big houses for if the dons married they would have families. A man brought up from birth in Oxford might not have seen the possibilities, but Walter had come from outside, and he had come to Keble College when it was half built. He realised that Oxford was on the brink of development.

The hardest problem was to get capital, for he had nothing and the only possible source was his mother, who was comfortably placed now but looked on speculation with great suspicion, especially if Walter suggested it. But he managed to get £600 and promptly took an option on a plot of land owned by St John's. The next step was to find a builder and here again his horizon was bounded by Keble College, which was put up by Parnells of Rugby. One of their foreman carpenters, Samuel Hutchins, stayed on in Oxford when the contract was finished, setting up as a builder on his own, and Walter asked Hutchins to get out plans, not for one house but three.

There was to be another stroke of luck. One day in college Walter heard that a new curate of the University Church had been appointed, so he caught the first available train to London and took with him the plans for all three houses, one of which had been built, one of which was going up and one of which had not even been started. Mr and Mrs Gorman lived in Clapton and Walter spent the afternoon with them. He must have had rare powers of persuasion for, when he said good-bye, he had sold them all three houses. They afterwards lived in one while the second was completed and the second while their final home was made ready. What was more, Walter laid the foundation of a friendship which culminated in his being made sole trustee of the Gorman estates. In his excitement on the afternoon of his first sale he walked all the way from Clapton to Paddington, stopping only to call on a tobacconist who on being asked for a cigar had the effrontery to offer him a sixpenny one. He might still look like a smoker of sixpenny cigars, he might talk like one, for he never lost his rustic accent, but he knew he had risen out of that class.

The Gorman deal was only a beginning. It provided him with capital and he knew how to get round the difficulties by making personal arrangements. For instance, St John's College owned land in North Oxford and stipulated that the plans must be passed by its own architect, so Walter employed the same man. When at last he felt confident enough to leave Keble he moved into a house which he sold to an investor by promising to become the tenant himself. But all his success depended upon his capacity to make other people trust him. This capacity had stood him in good stead with Colonel Shaw-Stewart, the Talbots and the Gormans. It was to make possible his relationship with the man who built most of the houses in North Oxford.

After the original houses had been built by Hutchins, the next contract went to a Mr Brucker and his two sons, but now he met the man with whom he was to form his most lasting business association. This was John Money, a builder of little reputation or substance before the partnership was formed.

The first contract between Walter and John was solemnised in a strange way. Until this time Walter smoked little and John not at all, but now the two men became compulsive cigar smokers and John succumbed to the luxury with such abandon that when he was on his death-bed he had a box of cigars put within reach so that, although unable to smoke, he could at least touch them. The contrast between the two men was striking. Walter was tall and stout. John was a thin little man about five feet tall. He always wore a silk hat and a long heavy overcoat even in the middle of summer. In summer he watched University cricket in the Parks and the most exciting occasion of his life was when Oxford beat the Australians. In winter, he went to every hunt in a hansom cab, the driver of which had orders to keep as near as possible to the hounds, so he was often closer than the field. It was not unusual to see the old gentleman clinging desperately to the cab as it careered through the middle of a wood in full cry.

This was the man whom Walter chose as his regular builder and this is what Walter's son wrote about the way they did business. "Once a week before breakfast, my father would walk to the building, accompanied by myself, then a small boy. He would walk round, ask the foreman a few immaterial questions and crack a joke with most of the men on the job. He appeared to take little interest in the buildings themselves.

"For the rest, he would rely upon two interviews each week with Mr Money. These interviews always took place at my father's house in the evenings on stated days of the week. Apparently the two never met at the buildings or elsewhere. On these occasions, Mr Money would arrive, not at the front door, nor at the back door, but at a side door. He would ring the bell at 6.30 precisely and wait for the door to be opened, when he would walk past the servant, unannounced, to a little general room. There, he would find my father in a very low, comfortable easy chair on one side of the fireplace, with his legs on another chair. If anyone else was present my Mother or my sisters, for instance, they would say 'Good evening, Mr Money', smile and instantly disappear. If I was present even as a boy of five, my father would say, 'You need not go, my boy'. In fact, neither my father nor Mr Money appeared happy unless I was playing in the room.

"Directly the room was empty but for me, Mr Money would say, 'Good evening, Mr Gray', and my Father would reply without moving from his comfortable position, 'Good evening, John'. John, without being invited, would take the easy chair on the other side of the fireplace, place his silk hat on the floor and very deliberately put a red handkerchief in the hat. He would then produce from his pocket a box containing a hundred cigars, saying, 'I have brought you a box of cigars'.

"Now this was the ritual on each of these meetings. It was not that Mr John Money gave my Father a box of cigars twice a week, but it was his job to buy my Father's cigars and keep him supplied.

"My Father would proceed to ask John Money a number of questions, to which he received quiet, conclusive answers and, by these questions and answers, my Father was kept in touch with the building progress. Next would sometimes come more important business. Without changing his position of comfort, my Father would pick up from the floor a roll of plans, which he would pitch across the room, to be caught by John Money.

"'I got these plans from St John's today,' my Father would say, 'what do you think it would cost to build a house like that?'

"John Money would look at the plans for about five minutes and say 'I should think it could be built for about £2,000', to which my Father would reply, 'Well, you had better get on with it, John; you had better see what Wild (the foreman) says'.

"And so the arrangements for building North Oxford proceeded, for my Father and John Money during their association never reduced a contract, however big, or any other matter to a written document. It was all trust between them covering transactions aggregating more than half a million of money.

"With John Money, in fact, it was all trust for he never put anything into a bank. When I cleared up his estate I found among the bags of nails in his cellar one bag of golden sovereigns."

2

Sensational Tory victory

IT took Walter very little time to discover that the important people in Oxford were not the Talbots, nor Dr Pusey nor, in fact, anybody in the University, but the men who were running the city or hoping to run it, and he had arrived just in time to join in a determined effort to overthrow the established order of things and institute a new régime. Oxford had always been a Liberal stronghold, which was not at all palatable to some of the local magnates especially the brewers, the Morrells and Halls, and it was A. W. Hall of Barton Abbey, always known as the "Little Squire" who put up as Tory candidate in the first election of 1874 when he was bottom of the poll to the two Liberals, Sir William Harcourt and Edward Cardwell of Army reform fame. The fact that the Tories could manage to put up only one candidate for the two seats was evidence of their weakness but they were not disheartened and ultimately, after a tremendous upheaval, and thanks largely to Walter Gray, they were to win through and make Oxford City safe for Conservatism.

The really important men behind the scene were two lawyers, Dayman and Walsh, who handled most of the local legal business and had important allies in the University. A visit to their office, according to Walter Gray, could be a strange and, indeed, unnerving experience because quite early in their partnership they had a serious quarrel after which they never spoke to each other again. They occupied two rooms separated by a narrow passage but when one wished the other to know something he shouted for Draper, the managing-clerk, who had a room at the bottom of the stairs, "Draper! Draper!", at which Draper would run up the stairs. Then, if it was Mr Dayman who had called, he would say, "Present my compliments to Mr Walsh and say so-and-so". This was said in a loud voice which Mr Walsh could plainly hear but Draper had to cross to the other room and deliver the message at which Mr Walsh would say in an equally loud voice, "Please thank Mr Dayman for his compliments. Present him with mine and say so-and-so", which Draper duly said.

It was with Gorden Dayman, much the older of the two, that Walter became friendly and in due time he was a regular guest at the old lawyer's house to which very few were ever admitted. The invitations were delivered in a surprising way for Dayman would suddenly appear outside the Gray house, hammer on the door and when it was opened shout, "Girl! Tell your master I shall have a leg of mutton on Sunday at 6.30: glad if he'll join me." The house, a beautiful Queen Anne building standing in four acres of ground behind an immense wall, was half a mile behind the city boundary and the approaching drive ran through a dark forbidding plantation. The carriage entrance was guarded by a ten-foot gate, covered with boards and anybody who succeeded in getting through the side-door had to undergo the scrutiny of the lodge-keeper before walking through a narrow passage and being let through a second door.

The lawyer's household consisted of a widow, Mrs Adams, and her two daughters, the lodge-keeper called Narroway, and a local man, Sturman, who helped Narroway with the gardens. Mr Dayman, if questioned about his housekeeper's children, absolutely denied their existence, and they were never allowed to be seen by him. As for the lodge-keeper, according to local gossip he had committed some crime known only to his employer, so now he had to do the dirty work. One of Narroway's jobs was to cure his master's colds, for when he came home with an uncomfortable head Mr Dayman would shout for the lodge-keeper in a stentorian voice, take off his hat, coat and collar, turn back the neck of his shirt, and put his head under the pump, while Narroway vigorously pumped the ice-cold water for a quarter of an hour. This was supposed to be highly efficacious.

At his office Mr Dayman never swallowed anything but tea but at home he had a sumptuous dinner, always with a bottle of burgundy. Before the meal, two clean napkins were put on the floor for his two dogs, Topsie and Tieman. At the beginning of the Sunday dinner when Walter and two other friends were present he ceremoniously placed a bottle of burgundy before each guest telling him to drink the lot or never darken those doors again.

There was something very odd about the house. Every door, inside as well as out, was fitted with eight bolts besides the ordinary lock, two piercing the floor, two piercing the ceiling and two running into the wall at each side, so that if a burglar ever got the lock and hinges off, the door would still be in position. There were no carpets on the floors, which were of polished oak, so that the slightest movement could be heard.

After dinner, when he went to his study, Mr Dayman stood for a few minutes over a table on which he kept a couple of loaded guns and, after Mrs Adams had brought in his coffee, he dismissed her and locked the door. It was in this room that he spent most of the night, and occasionally the clanging of shutters and the firing of a gun broke the silence; Mr Dayman had informed the world that the house was both armed and manned.

In summer, he stayed in the study until dawn; in winter he went to his bedroom at five a.m. Once a year a mysterious seafaring man paid him a visit and stopped a few days. Anxious to discover the reason for Mr Dayman's nocturnal habits, he sometimes asked permission to share the vigil, but his host invariably sent him to bed at ten o'clock.

Occasionally, there was a really large dinner party—for men only—and then he had the whole of his silver brought from the office in Oxford; after his death, it was sold for over £6,000. But his collection of linen gave him even more satisfaction.

Twice a year, an old packman left at the house an assortment of the best table linen, always including half a dozen napkins to match. Next Sunday, if weather permitted, Mr Dayman had the linen spread out on the lawn. Shouldering his stick like a gun, he marched round and round the assortment stopping occasionally to examine a cloth. On detecting a flaw, he flung the inferior article aside and, in this way, reduced the number to two.

"Mrs Adams!" he shouted, at the top of his voice, "Mrs Adams!"

His housekeeper having come out of hiding, Mr Dayman pointed to the linen with his stick.

"Now, Mrs Adams! I am much concerned and sore perplexed which of these two to have.'

Mrs Adams made a timid examination. "Well, Mr Dayman," she began, "I am not quite sure."

The lawyer glared, "Ah, Mrs Adams! You do not help me. You only serve to perplex me the more."

Desperately pointing to the nearer cloth, Mrs Adams said, "On the whole, Mr Dayman, I think I would choose this one."

"Would you," shouted her master, snatching the other one, "Then I shall have this."

Twice a year for forty years, on a fine Sunday morning, this comedy was played out on the lawn.

Mr Dayman had another house which proved useful as a hide-out when his difficulties in Oxford looked like becoming serious. It was at Dover and normally he went to it only one week in the year, in the hope of being able to see his native land across the Channel, for he was of French extraction. Like the famous President Routh of Magdalen, he never admitted that railways had been invented and for his regular week's holiday the old man left Oxford by wagonette on the day after St Giles' Fair which falls on the two days after the first Sunday in September. On one of these annual journeys his coachman behaved in such a way that he was afterwards threatened with an action for breach of promise which Mr Dayman had to settle at considerable cost. The incident was particularly annoying because he thought as little of women as steam-engines, and only two women visitors were ever known to have been admitted to his home.

Mr Dayman was no advocate and preferred not to appear in open court, but there was one occasion when he did so and that was to defend an earl and several members of Christ Church who had rounded up a number of cats in Oxford, taken them to Woodstock and hunted them with a pack of terriers. The R.S.P.C.A. issued a summons and, anxious to make an example of the distinguished undergraduates, sent down a Q.C. to prosecute them before the Woodstock magistrates. This lawyer made considerable play with the facts of the case, which nobody disputed, denounced the outrage in eloquent terms, and then proceeded to demand the heaviest penalty which was within the Bench's power to inflict. Mr Dayman was now called upon but to everybody's astonishment announced that he would offer no defence, after which the magistrates quickly brought in a verdict of "Not Guilty".

A curious explanation of the incident was offered by a radical London periodical, which had this to say, "Those who had the opportunity of hearing Mr Gorden Dayman's defence might be disposed to think that his very large fee had been very inadequately earned, but if the same persons had watched Mr Dayman drive on the previous Sunday from one magistrate to another, his personal friends and his professional debtors, they would be disposed to think that the fees had been more than earned". Perhaps it was because of this libellous comment that Mr Dayman retired completely into his shell and left the public part of the business to Mr Walsh.

Percival Walsh, the junior partner, was a very different character. A man of violent speech and energy he enjoyed nothing so much as acting a public part whether in the courts or as a political organiser. His original, no-nonsense conduct always impressed a new guest in his house for it was noticeable at dinner that, when the joint was carried in, it had been liberally carved already, since the servants were ordered to help themselves before bringing in the food. At the end of each course, if a guest was present Mr Walsh, instead of ringing for his servants, collected the dirty plates and remains himself, carried them to the door, put them on the floor outside and then rang for them to be taken away. If there was no guest he merely threw what was left on the fire. He said this method of clearing up as he went along was the only way to run a house and he would often dilate on the amount of money the country could save on refuse collection if everybody followed his example.

Mr Walsh showed his domestic originality and self-confidence in many other ways. Once, after enjoying an iced-pudding at a public banquet, he decided it was nothing but frozen blanc-mange which he would be able to prepare himself. For weeks he nursed his secret gastronomical passion and took a new interest in the weather. At last one morning, he saw the signs of a heavy frost, whereupon he sent several friends an invitation to dinner for that very night. The cook was ordered to prepare a large quantity of blanc-mange and Mr Walsh having inspected the delicacy told her to turn it out into fourteen large cups. He had decided that fourteen small blanc-manges would freeze more easily than one big one.

Just before the guests were due to arrive, he decided to have the blanc-manges turned out on plates which the family carried to the bottom of the garden and ranged along the top of the wall. In the dining-room a magnificent meal was served. As course followed course, the host could scarcely suppress his excitement. A guest would congratulate him on one of the dishes. "Ah," he would say, "Wait a bit! I've got a treat for you."

At last the time for the pudding arrived and everybody was ordered into the garden to receive the treat, but what they found was fourteen empty plates without blanc-mange. The cats had eaten the lot. One of Mr Walsh's sons guffawed at his father's discomfiture but thought better of it when he got a violent blow on his knee from a heavy stick and had to be put to bed for a week.

A man who would not trouble to consult his wife on the preparation of a dish for the dinner table was little concerned with the ceremonies and punctilios of public life, and Mr Walsh's swashbuckling conduct of the Conservative Party's affairs was to leave a permanent mark on the political complexion of the neighbourhood. He would stick at nothing to down the Liberals with whom he never tired of proclaiming himself "in deadly enmity".

He was Squire Hall's agent in the first election of 1874 when they were beaten and then, when they had the chance of fighting again in the same year, he launched his campaign by putting out a handbill addressed to the "Women of Oxford" which opened with the following question:

"Who said it would be better to dis-enfranchise Devonport than to repeal the Contagious Diseases Act?—John Delaware Lewis."

Remote though the issue must have appeared to Oxford, and particularly to the women who had never before been consulted about politics, it seized the public imagination. Passed ten years before, and designed to prevent the spread of venereal disease in naval and garrison towns, the Contagious Diseases (Women) Act, provided for the appointment of hospital inspectors and for penalties to be imposed on anybody who allowed prostitutes suffering from contagious diseases to use a room for prostitution. According to Mr Walsh, this meant nothing less than a system of legalised vice. "These Acts proclaim", he announced, "and the man who supports them endorses the statement—that a holy life is impossible for married men, and that women must be provided for them by the State." For if the State imposed penalties on anybody who let a room to a diseased prostitute, nothing was said about healthy prostitutes. What was this but a legalisation of vice?

Liberal newspapers quoted the medical and scientific testimony in favour of the Act, the report of the Royal Commission on this subject, the evidence proving that a frightful disease was being conquered and that "hundreds of young girls were being deterred from entering upon a vicious and abandoned career". Thomas Hill Green left his philosophic retreat in Balliol to point out "more in sorrow than in anger" that the condition of military towns arose from the custom of keeping men in virtual idleness and without opportunity of marriage, that women became victims of the bad passions of men because of the poverty and parental neglect arising from drunkenness, and that, if the local brewer should be elected to Parliament, there would be much joy in the public-houses but much sorrow in houses where domestic purity was held dear. But it was all in vain. In fact the Liberals were themselves divided on this burning issue, and Josephine Butler added to Mr Walsh's ammunition by describing the Contagious Diseases (Women) Act as "insulting alike to womanhood, to religion and to God".

It became so obvious that a Liberal victory would put an end to the sanctity of marriage that members of the party were openly assaulted on election day, and the local brewer won by 2,554 votes to 2,092; at which Mr Walsh declared, "God knows, since the day of my marriage, this has been the happiest day of my life".[1]

[1] 1874 was the year when Disraeli became Prime Minister replacing Gladstone, whose Ministry had lasted since 1868.

3

A political bombshell

THE election result was a frightful shock to the Liberals and especially to the older men who had inherited a great tradition and thought of themselves as omnipotent and infallible in Oxford. But times were unexpectedly changing (as ever) and what was most shocking was that a prominent Liberal could no longer count on his family or even his servants to follow his example and precept.

The Party was led locally by a solicitor's clerk, Alderman Richard Carr, known to everybody as Dickie. He took over the leadership from the famous Isaac Grubb who, when Mayor of the City, refused either to undergo the historic ceremony of humiliation to the University or go to Court to present an address of congratulation to Queen Victoria because they required him to go in Court dress and he had no mind to make a "Tomfool" of himself. Dickie Carr had been at the Liberal Association meeting of 1857 which refused to support the candidature of Edward Cardwell[1] on the ground that he was not radical enough, and put up Professor Charles Neate in his place, only to see Neate unseated on petition, with the result that Cardwell returned in triumph to defeat William Makepeace Thackeray. But it was in 1868 that Dickie Carr came into prominence for it was he who introduced Sir William Vernon Harcourt to the constituency.

[1] Later Viscount Cardwell (1813-1886). Became War Minister in 1868 and made his name by army reforms including abolition of the purchase of commissions.

Though a Radical in politics, Alderman Carr was a stickler for custom and one occasion he never missed when in good health. Every Sunday morning the members of the Corporation met in the Town Hall, put on their robes and, headed by the mace, set off for the City Church. When he was first Mayor of the city Alderman Carr introduced the custom of taking with him a box of sweet pastilles, one of which was presented to each member of the council so that as the procession made its way to divine service all could be seen vigorously chewing. At one time, Alderman Carr was seriously ill but he would not allow the custom to lapse and it became the duty of no less a person than the Chief Constable to call at the alderman's house, take delivery of the pastilles and see that they were distributed as usual.

Although Alderman Carr presided over the magistrates' bench with immense dignity there were times (according to Walter Gray) when his origins betrayed themselves, as when trying to test the word of a woman defendant he leaned forward with immense dignity and addressing a police witness said, "Constable, was you there or was you not?" to which the Constable replied, "I were". He played a considerable part in politics at a turbulent time but the most sensational story was that a bastardy summons was served on him when he was no less than 87 and when a fellow magistrate, hoping to reassure him, said "Well, of course it's impossible" he became very angry and paid a large sum as a matter of pride. He left a will so badly drawn up that two-thirds of his estate was dissipated in a great law action.

But what was most vexing was that he never succeeded in converting his own brother—who bore the remarkable christian name "President"—to the Liberal faith and he suffered great embarrassment in consequence. Once, on taking possession of a new house, Mr President Carr gave a house warming at which one of his friends said, "I wonder a great Conservative like you can bear to look at the tiles round your fireplace. They are the Liberal colours," at which Carr rushed out of the room, returned with a coal hammer and smashed the lot.

The difference between the two brothers was demonstrated most vividly at election times. Alderman Carr was never seen outside his home in any costume but a black tailcoat with a red button-hole, and a white waistcoat, which was made of flannel in winter and linen in summer. At election times, his brother also appeared in public wearing a tailcoat and white waistcoat but he wore the waistcoat on top of the coat, and in this ludicrous outfit paraded outside the alderman's house to show what he thought of him.

More indicative even than this, perhaps, of the subversive spirit abroad was the experience of another senior alderman, a certain Jason Saunders who started life as a page-boy and for a time was a footman but rose to a position of great affluence. He lived in Medley Manor in great style. It never occurred to him that his own servants could be anything but Liberal but he was to get a shock at the election.

Three weeks before polling day he said to the coachman: "Get the horses in good fettle and see the coaches are right; we've got to do the best for the cause." Confident that his staff supported the same cause as himself, he gave further orders on the day before the election, "Don't let's be afraid of our colours. Put plenty of ribbon on the horses and have them ready to start bringing the voters up at seven o'clock."

Next morning when he came down to breakfast the old Alderman was amazed to see his own maids flaunting the blue ribbons of the Conservative Party, and outside his horse and dog-cart almost completely smothered in blue. Rushing out of the house, he tore away the ribbons, rushed to a shop for red ribbons and drove the coach himself. But whenever he pulled up at a polling-station with a fresh supply of voters, his arrival was greeted by an outburst of booing from the bystanders, led by his own coachman.

The Liberals assumed that the world would return to its senses when Disraeli fell and Mr Gladstone came back into his own. Their candidates for the 1880 election in Oxford were Sir William Harcourt[1] and Mr Joseph W. Chitty who was a Q.C. but had the bigger advantage of having rowed four times for Oxford. The great weakness of the Tories was their shortage of cash, and

[1] Harcourt (1827-1904) had been one of the Oxford members since 1868.

though the Little Squire offered himself for re-election even Mr Walsh recognised they could not afford to give him a running-mate. There were only 6,000 voters in the constituency but getting a reasonable number to the polls and making sure of their votes was an expensive business for both sides. Before the campaign began, Sir William Harcourt proposed to Squire Hall that neither side should spend more than £2,000 and his opponent agreed. Percival Walsh thought this ridiculous. The Liberals had a bigger organisation and far more voluntary help; besides Mr Walsh would not trust them; he was at "deadly enmity" with almost every leading Liberal in town. But Squire Hall put his foot down and what was more told his agent he had agreed with Harcourt to cut out bills and placards of which there were far too many last time.

Mr Walsh fumed and scoffed at the agreement. The Liberals had already put up a "huge black placard" reading "Vote for Sir William Harcourt and Mr Chitty and the return of prosperity". Worse was to follow. Apparently Squire Hall had voted against the abolition of the "cat" in the Army with the result that the Liberals plastered the town with a caricature of the Squire actually flogging a soldier. From this moment the gloves were off. Still, it was generally agreed that, according to Oxford standards, the election was a tame one. On election day, a prominent Tory so far forgot himself as to pitch a bit of stout cardboard into a passing carriage and Lady Harcourt was struck in the face. A procession of Conservative donkeys was organised as a reply to a demonstration of bullocks organised by the radical butchers. The little Squire was freely advertised on sandwich boards as "No Place Seeker", "The Labourer's Benefactor" and (surprisingly enough) "The Soldier's Friend". One supporter backed him at three to one on, but he was bottom of the poll.

What followed proved a national sensation. When Mr Gladstone formed his new Government, Sir William joined the new cabinet as Home Secretary and this meant that he ought to seek re-election if his opponents required it. This was according to the constitution but it was not considered gentlemanly to make him stand again. Oxford's leading Conservatives were not so much

31

concerned about what was gentlemanly as what could be afforded, for funds had been exhausted by Percival Walsh's unsuccessful campaign. Dayman thought a new election would cost them not a mere £2,000 but twice as much, and that sort of money could not be raised locally. So an appeal was made to the Party leaders in London on the grounds that it would be worth the money to embarrass the Government by keeping the Home Secretary busy. A member of the Oxford Association, Mr Evetts, went up to London and met four Tory worthies, Sir William Hart Dyke, Colonel Talbot, Mr Skene and Mr Harvey, who were all spoiling for a fight but thought £4,000 a bit steep and eventually agreed to give £3,000. Evetts telegraphed to Oxford that he had gathered "bushels of corn", and returned to the city in triumph.

When he heard this, Mr Walsh hurried home in the highest spirits and cracked a bottle of champagne. Mr Dayman remained glum. He still thought £4,000 was needed to turn Harcourt out but after a conference with Evetts came down to £3,500 and went to Professor Montague Burrows, Chichele Professor of Modern History in the University, to ask him to start a whip round for £500. It was 10.30 at night when he reached the Professor's home and the Professor was out so he had to leave a letter. This was to provide a record in writing when the whole transaction came out in public.

Next day the Professor reported that the £500 would be forthcoming and the election was on. It was a bombshell, not only to Sir William Harcourt and the local Liberals but to the whole country. With the solitary exception of the *Globe* even the Tory Press was scandalised and *The Times* was blistering.

But national disapproval meant little in Oxford and particularly to Dayman and Walsh. Squire Hall, announcing the decision said he had "devilish near licked Cardwell and Harcourt in 1874"; he had won the seat and held it for six years, only to be used "infernally bad" by the publication of the cartoon depicting him in the act of flogging a soldier. He accused the Liberals of using "sadly unworthy means" to defeat him, so he thought it his duty to give the electors an opportunity to demonstrate their disapproval of a Government whose majority was unhappily built upon the foundation stones of "extreme Radicalism and Infidelity", and which "threatened disestablishment and Universal School Boards, accompanied by heavy School Rates and a Godless Education".

It was well known that the decision could only have been taken on the strength of London gold and fever began to grip the humble electors who thought it was meant for them. In the beerhouses it was said that bags of gold had been brought from London by a mysterious character called Matthews, otherwise Pegler but generally referred to as the "Man in the Moon". Children were told to look out for a tall man, about sixty years old with a grey beard, and ask him whether he was the Man in the Moon. The stories became more and more fantastic. In Nat Payne's beerhouse, it was said, a mysterious stranger declared he would pay every man liberally for his vote, but Nat treated him "very suspicious" and asked where the money came from, at which the stranger laughed and said he had taken his hat round in the Junior Carlton Club in London. In the poorer district of Osney, Thomas Wells, Manciple and Cook of Brasenose College, said he was asked by the stranger if he needed help in the shape of money, to which he said "That is just what we do want", at which the visitor opened a bag and said "Help yourself!" Up at the Summertown Committee Room, a man called on Councillor John Calcutt and left bags of sovereigns, with the words: "There is the money to pay for what has to be done", saying that one of the things to be done would be to employ men to paste Conservative bills over all the placards put out by the Liberals.

Whatever the truth about the Man in the Moon—and these stories were told afterwards by citizens anxious to prove how much they had been tempted—there were certainly some visitors from London, too many for Mr Walsh's liking. One was a certain agent William Snowdon, sent to Oxford by the Secretary of the Junior Carlton Club. Oxford was by this time in such a state of confusion that anything could happen. When he arrived at Oxford station, Mr Snowdon told a cabman to drive him to the headquarters of the Conservative Association, at which the cab-man said "Very good, sir", and promptly drove him to the Clarendon Hotel, the Liberal Headquarters. Here Mr Snowdon lost no time before going to the dining-room where he sat down to a juicy chop, but looking up in the course of this meal shud-dered to see a number of men wearing red colours and carrying staves, from which hung a number of large and small loaves. Liberals, by Jove! The arrival of Sir William Harcourt and his "lambs" increased the agent's bewilderment. But he stayed the night in order to spy on the enemy and try to discover a wearer of the red-and-white in the act of accepting a glass of drink without paying for it. Next morning Mr Snowdon went over to the Conservative Roebuck Hotel but was sent to another district and when he came back again was ordered out. Attracted by all the talk of gold the Conservative H.Q. was swarming with helpers and the story ran that the distracted Percival Walsh tried to get rid of the unwanted by sending them to distant wards with Secret and Confidential messages which read: "Send this fool on somewhere else".

It was all so flagrant that Sir William Harcourt consulted Joe Chamberlain, who got him to call in Francis Schnadhorst, Secretary of the Birmingham League. Mr Schnadhorst apparently knew all about corrupt electioneering, and when he arrived in Oxford brought with him a certain George Nuttall, well known as a personation agent. Their first step was to offer £20 for any information leading to a conviction for bribery and a placard was put out reading "In order to keep down bribery and corruption Sir William Harcourt and his friends have accepted the help of the well-known George Nuttall, who has detected sufficient cases to void any election".

Mr Walsh began telling everybody to be more careful, but disturbing stories reached his ears. For instance there was an enthusiastic Conservative called Stephen Peedell, landlord of the Prince of Wales' Inn, who called on a certain Edward Ambrose Teegan and asked how he intended to vote. The conversation, they afterwards agreed, went like this:

"You vote for the Squire," said the publican, "I will make it all right for you. I have been sent down here on purpose. You and Jack (Teegan's father-in-law) vote for the Squire and I will put a yellow boy in each of your hands."

He turned to Teegan's wife. "Look here, Polly," he said, "I will put a sovereign in each of your hands, if Ted and Jack vote for the Squire. What time does your father come home?"

Mrs Teegan said she did not know.

"See your mother", said Peedell, "And get her to persuade him, and neither of you will want through the winter."

"Well," said Teegan, "Look here, Stephen—who employed you?"

Putting his lips to the other man's ear, Peedell whispered the name of a great brewer, the Squire's chief ally.

"You hear that, Polly," said Teegan. "It's Mr Morrell! So it will be all right then!"

The publican became cautious. "Don't mention a word of this to anybody," he said.

"Well, all right, Stephen," said Teegan. "Shall I see you again tonight?"

"I might be down again," said the publican.

Stepping out of the house, he noticed Liberal bills in the window. "Get those bloody red bills down," he said, "What will Harcourt give you when you have voted? He will only thank you."

Later that night, the publican again called. "I have seen Mr Morrell again," he said, "And told him I have made you all right. He says you are a rank Liberal but, if I have made you all right, he will see that I am all safe in work. What will Harcourt give you? Nothing! So look out for your own benefit. You need not take the colours down, Mr Morrell says so, only be right on the day of polling. Above all, do not let that paper be seen, or both me and you would get into trouble, I told him you had a family coming. He said he would see you right."

On the paper was written a promise by which he, Stephen Peedell, promised "to pay E. A. Teegan twenty shillings on condition that he votes for Mr Hall".

But Edward Ambrose Teegan proved a particularly rank

35

Liberal for he went post-haste to Sir William Harcourt's rooms, told the whole story, and handed over the incriminating slip of paper. This sort of thing gave the Liberals great encouragement. They now started recruiting a band of "Liberal Association Guards", paying them five shillings a day to patrol the constituency and see that nobody was intimidated.

Meanwhile, the Liberal Press vented its spleen on Mr Hall. He was, the *Chronicle* maintained, "a gentleman who likes to pose sometimes as a fellow-citizen and brewer, sometimes as a country squire, according to the taste of those whose support he is soliciting, but who, even in these humble walks of life, has never achieved any particular notoriety; while, of any other distinctions that he has gained, whether academic or philanthropic, or otherwise, no whisper has ever reached us. True he has one rare merit, which, no doubt, gives him a great hold on the sympathies of many; he owns more public-houses than any one else in this City; and he is ably supported by a gentleman who is scarcely inferior to him in this high and enviable prerogative; and this, we presume, is the reason why two evangelical clergymen, whose names are always prominent on temperance platforms, are hoping to convert the two brewers to their own opinions and to induce them to shut one half of the public-houses under their control, in return for the aid and comfort they are receiving."

The two clergymen angrily explained why they were supporting the brewer's cause. One reason was that Mr Gladstone had appointed a couple of Romanists, one as Viceroy of India and one as Lord Chamberlain to Her Majesty the Queen. The other was that the two local brewers had promised to make tea and coffee available in their public-houses; in fact there was a distinct possibility that the publicans would agree to serve glasses of milk.

So far, in spite of all the excitement in the pubs and committee rooms, the actual election meetings had been comparatively mild, but now Sir Robert Peel, son of the famous Prime Minister, arrived to announce that if he could get near him, he would crumple up Sir William Harcourt "like a piece of paper", to which Sir William replied that Sir Robert has dissipated the inheritance of a great father, had changed sides more times than any man could remember, and was trusted by no man and no party. Sir William went further: the Tories, he alleged, were not depending on the eloquence and rhetoric of their assistants. "They have got a much more solid reserve," he said, "I might add that they have got a much more liquid reserve (laughter). Everything that money and that beer can do is being done, and will be done, in this City to turn the political judgement of the people of Oxford."

This theme was echoed in the national Press and *Punch* published the following:

Tory Brewer: The Conservatives are showing their mettle at Oxford.

Liberal Brewer: Yes,—base metal—though with the Hall-mark on it.

On the eve of the poll, there was a vast torchlight procession from the railway station to Sir William's hotel and his followers yelled the song written for the April election:

> Dare to be a Liberal,
>   Dare the cause to own,
> Dare to have a purpose firm
>   Dare to make it known.

> Harcourt and Chitty for Oxford!
>   Give them three times three!
> Send them both to Parliament,
>   And Hall to his brewery.

Sir William went on to the last holding up the brewers as bogey-men. "We know what this contest has been from the first," he said. "There is in this town at the present moment a band of brewers of England, who have come to buy the free votes of Oxford. You will show them tomorrow whether they can do it or not. Gentlemen! Mr Hall has been engaged in a shabby attempt, which he and his party are endeavouring to accomplish by dirty means. It will be for you to read him a lesson which he deserves."

Mr Walsh redoubled his efforts. He said that if anybody had a room to let it was to be taken. Over a hundred men were taken on as clerks, although there were only nine polling booths, and 250 messengers were paid to deliver between 50,000 and 60,000 circulars. Anybody not entirely paralysed could earn a few shillings by chalking Conservative slogans on the walls and pavements and then a few more shillings for rubbing out the Liberal slogans.

Fierce and irreparable quarrels broke out everywhere and President Carr was well to the fore.

"I will make it worth a fat pig," he said to Mr Godfrey the pork butcher, "if you will vote for Mr Hall."

"I never have," said the butcher, "and never will."

"You b——," said President, "I hope you'll be paralysed."

The mob surged through the streets shouting and hooting, breaking windows and pulling down flags and the police had to form lines down the middle of the roads in an effort to control them. Some of them, shouting and singing, marched to Beaumont Street, broke a window belonging to Professor Thorold Rogers and threatened to pull Dickie Carr's house down. When the police tried to take a prisoner to the station, the mob rushed them and seized the Superintendent. The city authorities sent urgent demands for police reinforcements to Bath and Leicester.

On election day it was not long after dawn when people started to come out of their houses and gangs of roughs gathered at the street corners. The first procession was of eleven boys wearing blue caps, who paraded in solemn single file, each bearing a single letter, and the whole legend reading "Hall or None" on one side, "Vote for Hall" on the other. A strange character, dressed in a Scottish cap and a blue gown, rushed along the main streets, incessantly imitating the sound of a bugle and stopping at intervals to frighten the women with what were called brutal grimaces. Soon after the polling booths opened there were rumours of personation. During the morning a red bill made its appearance to warn everybody that a man called Frank Hedges had been taken into custody for trying to vote twice but Mr Walsh, when he heard of this, swore it was a Liberal lie and had the walls plastered with posters announcing that Frank Hedges was not in custody but at work. Finally, the Conservatives drew a man round the city in a cart with a notice round his neck: "This is Frank Hedges."

Although the Vice-Chancellor had "gated" all undergraduates, many got out, wearing white coats, blue scarves and blue hat-bands. Apparently there was only one Liberal among them. Cabs crowded with men in blue rushed through the streets, stopping occasionally at a butcher's or grocer's shop to tear the Liberal bills down. More of Dickie Carr's windows were broken. The tumult was indescribable and the only lull occurred when Sir William Harcourt drove round the city hat in hand.

The Liberals were, in fact, still confident and Sir William's "lambs" made ready a couple of black coffins which they proposed to carry round the city after the declaration of the poll, with a mourning card:

> The mortal remains of old Toryism were consigned to their last resting place on Wednesday, 31st March 1880. The funeral cortège was formed at the cities, and passed through the boroughs of England and Scotland, old Ireland and Wales. A solemn oration was delivered over their mortal remains. The service was as follows:
>
> O, man that is born a Tory hath but a short time to live, and is full of humbug; he springeth up like a fungus, withereth like a cauliflower, and is seen no more; in the midst of life and hope he meets his death; O, Lord Beaconsfield, have mercy on their foolishness, and deliver them not again unto the bitter pains, and disappointments of elections, especially in the ancient city of Oxford. Forasmuch as it hath pleased our brethren here departed; we therefore commit their bodies to their own home, in hope of no return.

Polling closed at four o'clock in the afternoon, and the crowd began to gather outside the Town Hall. In the windows opposite, ladies bowed to the cheers of the people below, fluttered their little flags and screamed whenever they saw a scuffle in the street.

Inside the hall, Mr Gorden Dayman watched the counting on

behalf of Squire Hall, and thought it would be a very close thing. A leading member of the Tory Committee thought Sir William was in by 60 which went from mouth to mouth until it reached the mob in the street as an accomplished fact and caused an uproar. Somebody even proposed burning the Town Hall down. Then it became known that the contest was "worse than close". Alderman Galpin, the Mayor, reported that three ballot papers could not be accounted for but, in his opinion, the result must be declared without delay, or the crowd would get out of hand. Then somebody discovered the three papers had been put aside as spoiled.

At last the counting was finished and this was the result:

Mr Hall	2735
Sir W. Harcourt	2681
Majority for Mr Hall	54

Afterwards, outside the Roebuck Hotel, Squire Hall had to wait for ten minutes before he could make himself heard. He would not stoop to abuse his opponents, he announced, "It was not you or I that sought to upset the fair representation of this city, and, consequently, they have tumbled down, as they deserved to do".

As for Mr Walsh, he declared himself so much upset by the brilliant victory that he was unable, for the first time, to address his fellow-citizens without being propped up with brandy and water. This had been the first contest, he declared, that had not been embittered by a speech from Mr Percival Walsh.

Outside the Randolph Hotel, Sir William Harcourt's followers stood dumbfounded until their man came to a window. "My dear good friends of Oxford," he said, "for I call you so still, we have been defeated, but we have fought a good fight and in a good cause. We have done our best and that is all men can do. In the hour of defeat the true test of a man is to bear it manfully, as I hope you and I shall do. In the hour of defeat the worst thing in the world is to indulge in the language of recrimination. I have received too much kindness in Oxford for many years past to desire to leave behind me or to carry with me any sense of bitterness. I hope, gentlemen, you will go home in peace, as I shall go home in peace. I hope that after this severe and fatiguing contest you will sleep as I shall sleep tonight. My last words to you last night, gentlemen, were good night and God bless you, and I finish with the same words this evening—good night, and God bless you."

Still, Sir William[1] must have felt very strongly about it for he said he would never set foot in the place again.

[1] Harcourt found another parliamentary seat immediately. He became Chancellor of the Exchequer in 1886 and again in 1892. After Gladstone's retirement in 1894 he led the Liberals in the House of Commons.

4

The letter in the gutter

SOME of the Liberals immediately began talking about a petition. Their agent, George Nuttall, brought his men back from Birmingham, and told them to get more evidence, mix with the people in the public-houses and discover the names of people who had taken bribes. One of these Birmingham men, called Adams, had even got himself on to a Conservative committee, which he now reported had no genuine existence but gave an excuse for its so-called members to sit in a room all day long with a two-gallon can of beer provided by the Party. He had seen a lot of Conservative helpers being paid and asked them what they did for the money and this meant practically nothing. There was also the evidence of somebody called "Fidgetty Jim" who said he was paid 10s. for voting Tory, while another spy said that even Squire Hall's coachman had been heard saying he was afraid of being prosecuted for bribery.

Because of Nuttall's activity the Tories thought they ought to make their own inquiries into Liberal activities during the election and Mr Evetts proposed to consult a private inquiry agent in London called Nathaniel Druscovitch who sent down three of his agents, one of them introducing himself to the city as a commercial traveller, another as an actor and the third as a journalist, all deputed to discover scandals on the Liberal side. But Percival Walsh was as confident as ever and in fact rather more bumptious. During the hearing of a court case, Alderman Carr happened to make a remark to the Mayor and the Conservative agent took strong exception. "The reign of terror is over in this Court", he declared. Alderman Carr remonstrated against such language, at which Walsh said "My position in this matter enables me to regard what Alderman Carr says here or elsewhere with indifference". The right tactic, he thought, was to put on a bold front.

When he appeared to defend a publican charged with being drunk and trying to rescue a prisoner from the police, Mr Walsh demanded Alderman Carr's retirement from the Bench, because his windows were broken during the affray and he could not therefore be impartial. Alderman Carr refused, so Mr Walsh said he would leave the Court. "I think that is very improper," frowned the Mayor, "I must confess, Mr Walsh, I think your conduct very undignified." Mr Walsh promptly retorted that he expected no justice from that Court and, when called upon to withdraw these words, made the extraordinary reply, "I *think* I will withdraw them".

But even Mr Walsh had to admit it looked serious about that fellow Peedell, who had signed a paper promising to pay a sovereign for a vote. When a summons was served on him it was decided to get Peedell out of the way. Somebody discovered that the wretched fellow had had something wrong with his legs 15 years before. He had been in excellent health ever since, but how could he know the state of the leg under the skin? Maybe it was rotten, maybe the infection would spread and paralyse his whole body. Perhaps he ought to go into the Infirmary again and be operated on, preferably just before 21st May when the summons against him was due to be heard. This was the course of action proposed to Stephen Peedell who had been so stupid and might bring the whole Tory house down.

Suddenly the prosecution of publicans and personators and such minor actors evaporated like smoke simply because a boy, who was playing one day opposite the London and County Bank, saw a letter in the gutter and picked it up. It was addressed to the Public Orator of the University and this is what it said:

43

9 Norham Gardens
Oxford,
April 27, 8 a.m.

Dear Dallin,

I found a note from Dayman when I got home last night saying the fight must collapse unless we can provide £500 over the Carlton £3,000. By same post I got a letter from Hathaway saying he will come up and fight the election for us, and urging us to go on (from private information he has received of our good chances). Noel also promises to work Jericho[1] this time. I look on these two helpers as worth 100 additional votes. We are sure to win. The thing must be settled before 11 a.m. So I see nothing for it but to come forward and guarantee £50 myself on condition H. Morrell, Parsons and West bring £300 more by 11 today; but I must have help, and should like to raise my guarantee to £100. Can you aid me with £10 towards this sum? It is a crisis, and we must really sacrifice something for our party. Let me know by 10 a.m. at All Souls, or by 11 a.m. at Dayman and Walsh's office.

Yours sincerely,
M. Burrows.

The boy took the letter home and read it to his sister that night. His father, a small tradesman, who overheard them realised the importance of this letter and thought the phrase "Carlton £3,000" explained all the Tory money during the election, but he was in a dilemma because, if he made it public and the Tories suffered, they might get their own back on him. He must have been a man of conscience because he put aside such sordid considerations and sent the letter to the Mayor.

Now it was the Mayor's turn to scratch his head. The town clerk advised him to send a copy to Mr Dallin and invite an explanation, but Mr Dallin with remarkable effrontery sent back a stern note demanding to be told who had picked up the

---

[1] An Oxford district.

document. The brave Mayor refused to say and the tradesman's business was saved. What Mr Dallin should have been asked of course was whether he made a practice of throwing away important letters of this sort.

When it became known that this damning letter was in the hands of the authorities the Liberals were cock-a-hoop but Alderman Carr, surprisingly, was against launching a petition. He thought it would bring nothing but trouble. The others overruled him and, giving in with a good grace, he agreed to contribute £50 towards the expenses. Still, he always maintained it would not have been Sir William's wish.

So, early in June, a petition, signed by Thomas Hill Green and Dr Rolleston, Professor of Physiology, among others, was lodged against Mr A. W. Hall on the grounds of "bribery, treating, intimidation, personation and the employment of an excessive number of voters as clerks and messengers". Most of the leading Tories refused to believe that the Liberals would go on with it because their own dirty linen would come out, but they were wrong and Mr Justice Manisty and Mr Justice Lush were appointed to preside over the hearing.

The chief characters reacted by going into hiding. Mr Dayman retired to his house, ordered Narroway not to admit anybody and refused every summons to open in the name of the law. Mr Walsh took to his bed. A doctor's certificate was produced according to which he was not in a fit state of health to give evidence so officers of the law were sent to his house to take evidence and managed to get into his drawing-room. Presently he appeared in a wheel-chair, propped up with cushions, and the law officers began to question him, but they got nothing out of him for as soon as they put a question he sighed heavily and apologised but said he had had an awful illness and lost his memory.

For the moment these tactics were successful and the hearing opened without Dayman and Walsh. Counsel for the petitioners alleged that in ten days Mr Hall's agents had spent no less than £3,610, 12s. 8d., of which Mr Walsh had received 300 guineas as his fee.

The first witness was Daniel Higgins, a decorator. Mr Higgins maintained that he was approached by Joe Gynes, a compositor employed on the *Oxford Journal*, a weekly newspaper owned by Mr Hall's brother. Gynes asked Higgins whether he would give Hall a vote and said, "Is a fiver any good to you?" Later he gave witness 5s. and a port wine. On the Tuesday before the election, Gynes gave him a sovereign and witness reported the matter to the Liberal agents. Under cross-examination, he agreed that he was one of 296 "watchers" on the Liberal side.

Counsel: (for the defence) Do I understand you
                    were paid to lay traps for people?
Witness: No sir, I was paid to "ketch".
Mr Justice Manisty: He did not lay traps, he was the trap.
                    (Laughter)
Counsel: A baited trap. (Laughter)

Then came Thomas Stone, a wheelwright, who said he was approached by Mr William Anstey and was told to see Mr Benjamin Bennett, the dyer. On being asked for his vote, the wheelwright refused on the ground that he had been badly used by certain Conservatives; they had informed on him for coming out of hospital to vote in the previous election, with the result that he had been fined £1, 2s. 6d. by the Hearts of Oak Benefit Society. On election day, he said, Mr President Carr shook a bag of gold and silver in his face; the Conservatives were angry because they had not been able to buy his vote. The Judges next came to the case of Mr Dumbleton, the Conservative grocer, who was alleged to have tried a bit of bribing three days before the election.

"Who are you going to vote for?" Mr Dumbleton said to William Bowley, a road-sweeper.

"For Mr Harcourt," said Bowley.

"Well," said the grocer. "If you vote for Mr Hall, you will get five shillings; you will get nothing off Mr Harcourt."

The sweeper replied, so he maintained, that he would not sell his principles for all Hall's brewery. He denied that the conversation had been strictly about the brooms supplied by

46

Dumbleton to the local Board. It was alleged he had said, "They are first-raters; I have never seen such brooms for thirty years." "This could not be true," he informed the Court "I aren't been on the job but a year."

The next allegation was that Mr Dumbleton tried to seduce another man called John Jones, a plasterer, but fared even worse.

"I wants to see you," called the grocer at about two o'clock one afternoon. "Walk into my shop and wait there a few minutes."

Both men went inside and Mr Dumbleton said: "What do you think about the little Squire; do you think he will get in?"

"I really think he will," said the plasterer.

"You have been out of work a good deal this winter?"

"Not as I knows of."

"You have," said Mr Dumbleton. "You owes me a bill."

"Not as I knows of."

"Well you do. I'll give you half a sovereign and that shall stop the bill." As the plasterer took the money, his benefactor added: "I'm no paid agent, mind."

"I must have a little bill," said Jones, "to show that's done with."

"What am I to put down?"

"Sundry articles," said Jones, "such as grocery or anything else, from 1879 to some date in 1880."

The grocer began to scribble on some paper. "I must have your name," he said. "It's Clifford, is it not?"

"That's not my name," said Jones. "It's a lucky job this fell into my hands. I don't want to destroy your happiness."

Realising he had made a serious mistake, Mr Dumbleton tore up the bill, but John Jones thought he might get something else out of it so he went back to the shop later and said, "I want two ounces of tea, at the rate of two-and-six a pound, half a pound of plums and half an ounce of tobacco."

The grocer was furious. "Do you want anything else?" he shouted.

Benjamin Bennett was alleged to have approached a certain Henry Charles Hull, who lived with his grandfather, a tailor, in

George Street. "Good morning, Henry. It is no use asking you for your interest?"

"No," replied Henry, "it is not."

"Well," said the dyer. "We want to get the little man in this time. I'm afraid if we don't get him in this time, he won't stand any more. Can I speak to you in confidence?"

"Yes."

"If the old man is in want of a little assistance, I can give him a little bit of paper and, if he takes it to Mr Webber Paterson, it will be all right."

"No, thank you, Ben," Henry claimed to have replied. "We don't do things like that."

It appeared that the chief object in life to the cordwainer, Robert Dunsby, was to get his son elected as a freeman and, being in the habit of smoking a pipe at the Waterman's Arms in the evening, he seized an opportunity to mention the matter to an influential Conservative called Charles Linnell, who later took him into a back room and said,

"Now, you want your son's freedom?"

"Yes."

"That would be 7s. 6d. and if I give you a pound, that will be all right. I will give you a pound if the Squire gets in."

After the election, it was alleged, Dunsby was promised £2 but then they turned against him and accused him of having mentioned the matter to a Liberal agent. It was a fact he had had a few words with Mr Nuttall at the Alliance Temperance Hotel but, as for the counter-allegation that he had been after the Liberal reward because he had lost money on Von der Tan in the Derby, that was a lie.

What struck the judges most forcibly was that everybody in the witness-box claimed to be blameless. A certain Charles Ives, on being offered £10 for the use of his house as a committee room—the rent he paid being only £13 a year—said he replied: "How could I do such a thing—just turning; having been on the Liberal side two or three months ago?"

Thomas Langford, a labourer when offered three half-crowns to act as a messenger for "the little one" said he refused because "he did not want the money; there were plenty of men about the streets who would be glad of the job".

Before the audience had fully recovered from this, Thomas Wild, a railway-porter, told his story. He said he was button-holed by a certain George Porter at the Great Western Station.

"Mr Wild," said Porter, "I know you are a man of your word, and if you promise me a thing you will do it. Will you promise me you will vote for Mr Hall if I give you half a sovereign?"

"Certainly not," said Thomas Wild. "We vote by ballot and I won't have anything to do with any bribery."

Mr Justice Lush congratulated the railway porter on his honesty. Tom Wild had saved the honour of the city.

But unhappily a labourer called John Padbury had almost succumbed to temptation.

"Have you got any pigs?" John Padbury was asked by Thomas Cleaver in Peedell's public-house one night. He had known Cleaver for thirty years, and regarded him as a "bit of a joking covey".

"Why?" he asked.

"You can have two sacks of barley-meal on the cheap", said Cleaver.

"No."

"You can have a pound or two."

Padbury put his hand out. "Let's have it," he said.

"I haven't got it," said Cleaver. "Go along with me in the morning and you shall have it."

Padbury's hopes fell. He would have taken it if it had been on the spot, he declared, but it was "easy enough to change his mind in a moment".

"I now say," he informed the judges, "I would not have taken the money because I knew Cleaver had not got it."

Inspired by this remarkable declaration, the Conservative Counsel, Mr Matthews tried to have a little fun with John Padbury who had apparently received his subpoena from Joe Richards of the "Bird in Hand".

"Did Mr Richards give you that hat," asked Mr Matthews, amid loud laughter, "to come to Court in?"

"No," said Padbury with some heat. "What's that to do with it? He never give me anything, not so much as a half-pint of beer."

So Padbury had retired, with his remarkable hat, and then the foreman porter at the railway station admitted that, on being offered half a sovereign for his vote, he said: "I don't think you have more half-sovereigns than you know what to do with but, however, if you can give me half a sovereign out of your own pocket, perhaps out of Mr Morrell's thousands you can get it made up to a sovereign."

Certain allegations were then made against Mr Wheeler, the coal-merchant. "If they can afford to give £10", he said to a plumber, "we can afford to give £15." In the Britannia beer-house one night, a customer hailed him with the words, "All right, Mr Wheeler, we shall pull it off this time." "I think we shall," Mr Wheeler replied, putting some money on the bar, "I have not got much money with me; here's the price of two quarts of ale." An unemployed labourer, who happened to be present, swaggered about after the election with some gold in a "bacca box", because he had been taken on as a messenger at 5s. a day.

There remained Charles Walker to restore the moral reputation of the city for, asked by the Conservative counsel if he was a Liberal, he heatedly retorted, "That I am not obliged to tell everybody." He said a publican in a village a long way away offered him 15s. and all his expenses to paint "a couple of little sashes and whitewash a little ceiling" but it must be done on Saturday, 8th May, which happened to be polling day, and he must not return to Oxford before five o'clock in the evening, an hour after polling finished. Walker indignantly refused, so he maintained. "I would not lose my vote," he asserted, "for £20."

The testimony of these small fry produced an effect because the more important men in the background began to realise what they were up against. Either Mr Hall would have to resign the seat, or the most damaging revelations of his affairs would be made public and there might even be criminal prosecutions. So the Tories decided to bow to the inevitable.

They told their counsel to throw in the towel. Mr Hall would no longer contest the petition and it would be for their lordships to declare the election void. Probably the transactions of Messrs Gynes, Bennett and Wheeler could be established but Professor Burrows was not an agent for Mr Hall and the contents of his letter savoured of common-room gossip (whatever that might mean). The employment of the messengers could be justified on the ground that the Post Office would not have been able to deal with the 50,000 circulars sent out in answer to the Liberal caricature of Mr Hall in the act of flogging a soldier; furthermore, there had been a great deal of work in rubbing out the enemy's slogans on wall and pavement. Still, Mr Hall felt it to be his duty to his own character, when corrupt practices had been established against persons for whom he was responsible, not to waste their lordships' time by continuing to contest the petition.

5

Disfranchised

THE decision by the Tory bosses to throw in their hand was obviously taken in the hope of keeping the dirtiest linen in their cupboards, but they had annoyed the Government and so had to pay the full penalty. A Commission was appointed, consisting of Lewis M. Cave, Hugh Cowie and Edward Ridley and one of its more curious aspects was that the third of these gentlemen had been a contributor to Mr Hall's campaign. When the news of this commission became known, Mr Dayman thought all was lost and, summoning his wagonette, drove post-haste to Dover, hoping to put himself out of harm's way. But the Commissioners wanted to know everything and so they offered an indemnity on certain terms. "If we are satisfied", they announced, "that witnesses called before us, honestly tell us all they know about the matter, we are empowered, and indeed required, to give them a certificate of indemnity which will be a most effective protection to them against the consequences of any illegal acts which they may have to acknowledge hereafter." This was considered very decent and the first to take advantage of the offer was Percival Walsh who had claimed to be at death's door, and to have lost his memory to boot.

When he made a miraculous appearance in court, apparently in the pink of health, he was asked to produce the receipts for all the expenditure.

"Nearly all the papers", Mr Walsh declared, "were destroyed

six or seven days before the petition. They were destroyed by my directions. I had my reasons for it." And when asked what were the reasons he replied, "They would probably have disclosed *quasi* corrupt practices. They would have demonstrated to you my accounts could not have been kept right."

He said that his clerk, Draper, kept the accounts but he wanted to protect the "poor fellows" employed on the Conservative side from a criminal prosecution and so asked for the destruction of the vouchers. Mr Walsh admitted that no less than 204 messengers and 41 clerks had been employed and then remarked, "The employment, no doubt, was excessive".

When he was asked about Professor Burrows's letter he said only £2,700 of the money from London had come into his hands but he thought his partner had had the balance. They received an additional £1,000 from subscriptions in London and borrowed £500 in their joint names. Over £500 was given them by Mr Evetts in order to pay debts standing over from past elections. But what did these details matter? "It was a mere juggle," he said, "to pay illegal expenditure."

Some of the money they gave, "for corrupt purposes", to Mr Matthews of Brighton, the gentleman who took the original cheque to London and changed it into gold. "And who was Mr Matthews?" asked the Commissioners. "An electioneerer," said Mr Walsh, "the man who stayed six days to see that we were doing our duty." Other witnesses said Mr Matthew's real name was Pegler; some said he lived in Brighton, some in Hastings; later, the Commissioners identified him as a linen-draper in Leeds. An officer who tried to serve a summons on Mr Matthews (or Pegler) in Rutland Gate, London, thought the wanted agent had fled to Stratford-on-Avon, but there learned from his brother that he had gone to Bradford in Yorkshire. Finally, they thought he had escaped to the continent. Failing to discover the whereabouts of the "Man in the Moon", and embarrassed by the total absence of Conservative accounts, the Commissioners settled down to a lengthy stay in the city.

They were helped considerably by Mr Walsh who was only too ready to make a clean breast of it. "Not one single account

I have published", he announced, "is approaching accuracy." At the same time, he must say a word about his political opponents. The case against him, he alleged, was contrived by those Birmingham roughs. "The manner in which the Liberals obtained their evidence was to go round to the lower class of voters with a bright blue portrait of Mr Hall, and ask how much they had received for their votes, under the pretence and promise they would see Mr Walsh and try to get more." What was more, he must say a word about the authorities of the city. The returning officer was a Radical and fixed the polling stations with the purpose of giving the Conservatives the greatest possible trouble. The registers were shockingly kept.

"Every authority in the town," said Mr Walsh, "is opposed to my own party. I now say that I suffer from a tyranny as intense as ever existed in any town in the country."

The Commissioners said it had been suggested that the Tories actually put out forged ballot papers which could be distinguished from the genuine papers by the fact that Mr Hall was described on them as occupying "Barton Lodge", instead of "Barton Abbey".

Mr Walsh said certainly he used imitation ballot papers not only in Parliamentary but in municipal elections. It was to teach ignorant people how to vote. When he heard that Mr Bickerton, the Liberal agent, was trying to discover who had ordered these facsimile papers, he advised the printer not to say anything. But it was an absolute lie that eight of the imitation papers were found in the ballot box, marked with Conservative crosses.

"Good God!" he exclaimed at one point, "Accusations have been founded on these things that are enough to drive a man mad!"

He remembered that Mr Evetts had pointed out a very curious fact about those ballot boxes. The counting of votes was completed on a Saturday night; yet the boxes were not sent to London until the Monday morning. Afterwards there was the rumour that forged papers had been found in the boxes. Since no forged papers were discovered on the Saturday night he would like to ask how did the Liberals discover such a thing afterwards? They must have opened the boxes. In fact, he suggested that the Liberals kept the boxes back in order to go through the voting papers and make a black list of all who had voted Conservative. He demanded an inquiry into a gross breach of the Ballot Act. The Commissioners tried to satisfy him by calling upon the Mayor, who testified that the ballot boxes were not touched after the original counting and that no forged papers were found in them.

Mr Walsh now made his most sensational confession.

"When the election was over," he said, "and Sir William Harcourt was defeated—which I confess astonished me—I knew what fate awaited me, and I immediately gave orders that the papers be burnt as speedily as possible, and that no lists should be sent to me, and having thus protected myself, I sat down to see what could come."

Everybody laughed, and he added: "I have placed myself in an unmeritorious light, and I am exceedingly anxious, if I can discover any merit in myself, to show you what it is."

Asked if it had been in Mr Hall's interest to employ corrupt practices, he replied, "Certainly, or I should not have done it."

"That is to say," said one of the Commissioners, "you could not win without?"

"I never," said Mr Walsh, "fought a pure election in Oxford in my life."

Presently, he recovered his spirits sufficiently to make a renewed attack on the Liberal authorities. Both the presiding officers and the magistrates, he alleged, were generally corrupt. Most of the voters were labourers and, in the polling booths, they came face to face with men who had been canvassing in the Liberal interest. In his opinion, a vote for the Tory candidate was sometimes refused.

The Commission had scarcely recovered from the shock when Mr Walsh changed his mind. Because he had no direct evidence of corruption on the part of the presiding officers and magistrates, he announced, he would withdraw the charge.

"It is impossible." protested Mr Cave. "You make a charge of corruption and then withdraw it!"

On his next appearance, Mr Walsh was all contrition. "I have been exposed," he said, apologising for his recent accusation, "to an amount of distress in body and mind during the last seven months which I think very few have been subject to. At the hands of the Commissioners, I have been exposed to an ordeal I think most men would think worse than death itself."

At this point, Mr Gorden Dayman returned from Dover and was put in the witness box. It must have been a severe ordeal for a man who hated publicity.

No, it was impossible for him to recall when he had first heard of Mr Hall's intention to contest the seat. Perhaps it was the result of a meeting on the 21st of April. Of course he did not participate in the meeting himself; his visit to Mr Evetts' house was an accident, the purest accident in the world. He expected to learn the result of the discussion from his partner but, failing to do so, he went down to inquire about it and was asked to remain. It was unfortunately true that, on walking home, he called on Professor Burrows and left the note to which reference had been made; but the reason why he stipulated for an additional £500 was in order to pay off the debts standing over from past elections. Indeed, when he afterwards paid Mr Wells and Mr Calcutt, he made it quite emphatic that the payment was for old debts and not for the current election.

As for the cheque brought by Mr Evetts from London, he could not say he remembered having it at all; it might have been handed to him, but he had no recollection of receiving it. True, Matthews or Pegler—or whatever he called himself—came to the office with no less than 3,000 sovereigns in bags; but why should he bring them to his, Mr Dayman's, office? That is what he asked. Some members of the committee had directed him there, Mr Matthews replied. But he, Mr Dayman, declared flatly and finally that he would have nothing to do with the money. Indeed, he sent across to the ironmongers immediately for a tin box—at a cost of twelve shillings—put the gold into it and gave the key to Matthews, who took the box to the bank in the company of Mr Draper. As for Mr Walsh's suggestion that he, Mr Dayman, had £300 of the money, that was quite a mistake. True, he offered to liquidate the debts which certain gentlemen had contracted in previous elections, but not out of money from London. Indeed he spent £400 belonging to Messrs Dayman and Walsh.

Unfortunately for Mr Dayman, his own Clerk, Draper, testified that he received the original cheque from his master, who said he was to hand it over to Mr Matthews.

"I very much doubt," Mr Dayman interrupted, "whether I gave the order."

For a moment, his evidence carried some weight, since Mr Walsh had refused to touch so dangerous a slip of paper and "did not presume to get it changed into cash". But the Commissioners pressed Mr Dayman.

"All I did," he conceded at last, "was to receive it, but further I do not know anything about it."

Describing his visit to the Conservative Office, Mr Evetts had mentioned that he talked the proposal over with Mr Dayman. The old lawyer quivered.

"I have no recollection of the cheque," he maintained again. "I have no doubt I was annoyed at the cheque being sent to me, as I was not Mr Hall's agent, and it had nothing to do with me whatever."

A few minutes later, the Commissioner extracted a striking admission. "My recollection as to receiving this cheque," he said "is very faint now. I fancy I must have seen this cheque in opening the envelope."

The Court laughed and he made an attempt to cover up his confession. "I have taken no active part in any previous election," he assured the Commissioners.

"Considering that you seem to have nothing to do with the election," Mr Cave dryly remarked, "it seems singular that you should have been entrusted with such a large sum of money." Mr Dayman stepped down.

His junior partner on being recalled said they both "kicked up a great row" because the cheque had been sent to their office.

"If it was for the purpose of the election", he was asked, "why should you be afraid to have it pass through your hands?"

"Do you think", he said, "that £3,500 could be for legitimate expenses?"

This attempt by the judges to pin down the men chiefly responsible was interrupted on several occasions. One witness applied for the protection of the Court, because, he said, whenever he went outside the Court somebody challenged him to a fight. A venerable Liberal Alderman, Mr Randall, complained of "a person of the name of Washbourne West, a reverend divine, a clergyman of the Church of England, a Master of Arts and, I am sorry to say, a member of the University of Oxford, who had said, 'There are other ways of corruption besides money. I refer to an Alderman who has been a Conservative and votes Radical; I mean Alderman Randall, who did this to keep his gown.'" Called upon to justify the remark, the divine said, "It is a notorious thing that Alderman Randall is pointed out as a turn-coat", but the distracted Commissioners ruled that this was a red herring and immediately afterwards a man in the body of the hall dropped down in a fit.

Another sensation was the convenient death of Mr Dallin, Public Orator, but not even this saved the really important Tories from public examination. Now Mr Morrell the great brewer had to give evidence. He tried to blame it all on Alderman Carr, who said before the April election, "We don't care to oust Mr Hall altogether, but we must have an election for the benefit of the town". This made Dickie Carr purple with indignation. He said no such thing! On the contrary, an election "was one of the worst things that could happen to a town, except to a few individuals". And what did Mr Morrell himself say, Dickie Carr would like to know. "He did not wish to be unjust to any foe, but when they tried to let loose upon them, as on a previous occasion, a man more like a Red Indian than anything that was ever seen, it was about time they took the thing in hand to see, if such another came, he was tarred and feathered." That is what Mr Morrell said and people afterwards called him the Jingo of Headington Hill because of his closing remark, "We don't want to fight but by Jingo if we do!" By the "Red Indian" Mr Morrell meant John Delaware Lewis, the gentleman who stood in the Liberal interest in 1874, and what was the speech but a direct invitation to the mob to tar and feather Mr Chitty? It was in consequence of his determination to prevent such an outrage that he, Dickie Carr, as Chairman of the Police Committee, brought in extra police from Birmingham. Had he not been justified?

One confession Alderman Carr felt himself forced to make. The amount of colours used during the election was utterly shameful. The public appetite was such that on one occasion he, himself, actually took the red and white necktie off his own person and gave it to an unknown fellow in the street. People demanded flags and, unable to resist their importunity, he spent £13 out of his own pocket. Alderman Carr became pathetic, "I know now that expenditure was illegal," he said, "and, unless you give me a certificate, somebody will prosecute me."

After this confession, the Commissioners decided to adjourn to London, where they hoped to find light to throw on the corners which were still dark. But they were disappointed. Nothing more could be gathered about Matthews alias Pegler. All that Colonel Talbot, Sergeant-at-Arms of the House of Lords and chiefly instrumental in financing the election, knew about the "Man in the Moon" was that the Secretary of the Junior Carlton Club had introduced him as a retired business man. "Yes," confessed the Colonel, "Pegler came to the club to explain that the cashing of the cheque for £3,000 in Oxford would reveal that Mr Hall was not fighting with his own money and so Matthews asked could the cheque be changed into one negotiable for cash." Certainly! To a man he had never seen before, Colonel Talbot entrusted a new cheque which was promptly turned into 3,000 sovereigns at Drummonds' Bank.

But the Carlton Club, said the Colonel, had no responsibility for the transaction. Then where had the money come from? Ah, that Colonel Talbot could not say; nor could anybody else. All that could be discovered was that the Junior Carlton Club made a grant of £500 after the election to help Mr Hall in fighting the petition. So, Mr Martin, Secretary of the Club, ought to be called before the Commissioners, but where was Mr Martin? Nobody knew. "I am going away for a few days", he informed his assistant on learning that the Commission had gone to Oxford and Mr Martin was still away. In fact, he failed to return.

There was a long series of sittings at the House of Commons, during which the Commissioners succeeded in unearthing only two scraps of concrete evidence: one, the Junior Carlton Club bought its linen table-cloths from a certain Charles Pegler; the other, a certain John Ramsbottom, of Lancashire, on visiting Oxford after the election and finding Mr Walsh struggling to make his accounts square at midnight before the day for sending them in, signed a receipt for 200 guineas, which he had never seen. No further evidence could be obtained. Entirely baffled by the stony front of the Conservative Central Office, the Commissioners packed their bags and returned to Oxford.

Here, the standard of entertainment returned immediately to its former level.

"What are your political views?" Mr Ridley asked one witness.

"That's a question," replied the witness.

"What were the colours you wore?"

"I wear either colours," replied the witness.

"Which did you wear in April?"

"None."

"Which in May?"

"The same, sir."

Another witness, one of the Conservative messengers, declared roundly that he "voted independently of the employment and went the way his bread was buttered, and at both elections pleased both parties; he promised nobody and voted according to his conscience". Fidgetty Jim appeared to say he thought "voting best left alone and then neither party could be offended".

After 38 days the inquiry drew to a close.

The length of time occupied by their labours, Mr Cave announced, could be ascribed to Mr Walsh's destruction of the Conservative accounts. During the elections of that year, a sum of about £10,350 had come into the hands of the Oxford Conservative Party and, of this, some £1,700 remained unaccounted for. Between 800 and 900 were charged with receiving

60

bribes. On the advice of the Commissioners, all the principal agents of the Conservative Party were scheduled; and Oxford was disfranchised for seven years.

After the closing of the Commission in January 1881, the city experienced the worst frost for fourteen years, a snow storm of unexampled ferocity paralysed business for two days, gables fell from houses, a few poor lives were lost, no trains or newspapers could be brought through from London. Dr Acland's carriage sank in a mountainous drift.

Every true-blue felt it was a judgement on the Liberals.

6

The Mighty Samson

W HETHER Walter Gray was entirely responsible for
thinking out the way to discredit the Liberals and make
Oxford a Tory city was never known. It is certainly a fact that
he had the assistance of Mr Morrell the brewer and Mr Dayman
the lawyer, and it may be that they thought up the plot together.
But it seems odd that Walter, a comparative newcomer, should
have been given the chief part and it is more likely that he started
the ball rolling, after which the others joined in to get the
maximum advantage.

The idea was to discredit the biggest savings bank in the city
and so ruin the people who ran it, that is the Liberals. The bank
was the Oxford Building and Investment Company which
started in 1860 with a capital of £25,000 which grew in twenty
years to £300,000 and which financed building development
over a wide area stretching as far as Swindon. In 1881, when
Walter first got himself elected to the City Council, he bought
a £25 share in the company in order to get its balance sheet and
accounts. There was a slight recession but the Society was still
sound. When he had finished with it the Society was in ruins
and so was the Liberal Party.

The squabble started on a bitter personal note which gave it a
peculiar interest. Immediately after joining the City Council
young Walter Gray was put on the Finance Committee and was
snubbed for his inexperience. The man who snubbed him was

Alderman Galpin, an ex-Mayor and Secretary of the Building Society, and Walter determined to get his own back. In fact, Alderman Galpin became his chief target and the attack became more and more libellous, not stopping short of the allegation that the Galpin family were guilty of corrupt practices.

Although he was so new to municipal affairs Walter must have impressed his seniors for he was asked to speak at a Conservative dinner and decided to get some publicity. He declared that Oxford was run by "the Building Society clique headed by the chairman, Alderman Cavell, and they were far too secretive about what was going on". Although no orator, he became quite rhetorical and said that, while no doubt a properly conducted Building Society was a good thing, it was very painful when the terms were harsh and severe, when they saw it drag down one poor man after another, and saw them wandering about the streets like lost sheep! If they would look at the neglected and forlorn and decayed state of Wellington Square, Tackley Place, and Osney, where something like three and twenty houses and many other places were empty, they would find some thousands and thousands of pounds locked up, and money was being daily and daily wasted. If, after that fearful waste of property, the Company could pay a large dividend, and large salaries to its officers, then nothing but the extraction of the most severe and harsh terms from the unfortunate borrowers could do it. Those huge and hideous masses of ugly brick, which had been raised up under the auspices of the Oxford Building Company, were in his opinion a disgrace to Oxford.

Having electrified his audience by this attack on an almost sacrosanct institution, Walter warmed to his main task of demolishing Alderman Galpin, who had dared to snub him in the City Council. Not to put too fine a point on it, he accused Alderman Galpin of feathering his own nest.

It was quite right for the officers—he did not say one word as to the zeal of Mr Alderman Galpin—it was quite right that they should study the shareholders as long as they did not injure anyone else. He was quite sure that a better man never lived than Alderman Cavell, and he was quite sure it was painful

63

to Alderman Cavell to know that he received the profits of his large stake in the Building Society when he knew that they were extracted "with many a sigh" from many of the poor. He thought he would not be wrong in any of his facts, and on the night previous he had a long interview with a poor unfortunate brewer, who told him chapter and verse everything connected with it, and said he was prepared to state it upon his oath.

The poor unfortunate brewer said that he wished to build a couple of houses, and on asking for a loan he was told that he would want some plans, and for these he was charged eight or ten guineas. Then the brewer was told that he could be supplied with timber, and in this way profit No. 2 was realised. Mr Galpin was also the Secretary of the Oxford and Berkshire Brick Company, and when the brewer was supplied with bricks there came profit No. 3. Then, of course, the Secretary of the Building Society had a commission upon all loans.

He was not going to say for a moment but that Mr Galpin acted with the full and free sanction of the Directors, but what he would say was this, whether Mr Galpin acted with their full and free sanction or not, if it was not a corrupt practice it was an undesirable one. What he considered was the most undesirable part of it was that Mr Galpin certified on property in which he had an interest in the timber, bricks and plans, and he was a fool if he did not certify sufficient to satisfy himself.

In his slow, heavily accented voice Walter went on to elaborate his argument by describing another means by which his enemies tried to mulct the unfortunate brewer. There would be a certain cheque, he said, drawn in favour of the advance which the brewer applied for, and duly certified; but, before it was handed to the unfortunate brewer, they said to him, "My dear sir, we shall require to draw on account of timber tomorrow". On another occasion, it would be the brick account that they would have to draw for, with the result that, when the unfortunate wretch went on Saturday to take his money, he did not receive the amount he had applied for, and which had been voted by the Board of Directors. The man he had alluded to most positively

Sir Walter Gray as Mayor; "Father of Oxford Conservatism".

assured him that cheque after cheque of his had been passed through the bank by Mr Galpin and, in the end, he had been paid some miserable amount, after deductions had been made on account of timber, bricks, etc.

Walter was surprised at the way his speech was received. The attack had been on the leading Liberals so his Tory audience ought to have been pleased, but on the contrary some had visibly paled. The fact was that quite a few of them had their money in the Building Society and what Walter said made them extremely nervous. Even Mr Morrell, the "poor unfortunate brewer" was thoroughly alarmed and said, "Do you want to ruin thousands of poor creatures?" He advised that the newspapers should be asked to suppress the speech and Walter, not entirely sure of himself yet, tried to get it suppressed.

Nevertheless, reports of the speech went around and started a panic. Everybody could see that many of the Society's houses were empty and people began taking their money out. At the next annual meeting of the Society, the Chairman had to announce a reduced dividend and made a gloomy speech saying "it was more than probable that without much caution and discrimination they would not have been enabled to declare a dividend". The Vice-Chairman said: "I suppose if the most flourishing concern in the world was at once set upon, and all those who had claims upon it wanted their claims settled on the instant, great loss would entail on the company; it could not be endured and nothing could stand it! I suppose the Bank of England could not stand it."

There was only one thing to do, go into voluntary liquidation, to which the shareholders agreed, for assets were so enormous that every creditor could be paid in full, confidence would be restored and the Society could start up again. But it was a staggering blow to the authorities, in other words the Liberal Party.

"We are guilty of no exaggeration", said the *Oxford Chronicle*, "when we affirm that no event in the memory of the present generation has produced such a painful sensation throughout the city and neighbourhood. Mr Gray claims to be the mighty Samson who has pulled down the industrial structure which had

65

its headquarters in New Inn Hall Street. Mr Gray is said to be a dabbler in house-building on his own account, but whether these speculations have proved as successful as he could have wished is a matter about which we make no conjecture."

It was a battle of wits. Voluntary liquidation did not fit in with Walter's plans. The Society proposed to appoint a London accountant as liquidator and the company claimed that they had assets of no less than £272,000. They put out a statement according to which "the company is solvent in the sense that all its assets, if realised with prudence and caution, might be more than sufficient to pay its liabilities". Walter now opened up a campaign to prevent the appointment of anybody nominated by the company on the ground that this valuation of £272,000 ought to be investigated by an outsider because it was probably a false one. He went to extraordinary lengths to prove that the Society's directors were thoroughly unreliable and, since he was never prosecuted for libel, there may have been something in his allegations. He said he could "prove that £500 never left Mr Galpin's office". Mr Galpin had bought some land in his own personal name and the sale of plots of land had secretly been arranged among nominees. Some of Mr Galpin's speculations he described as "curious and amusing" and he claimed to have documents and vouchers from the Secretary's office to prove it. He must have had inside information.

The important people were the bondholders and Walter knew some of the most substantial. They now got together to denounce voluntary liquidation as a trick to save the directors from an inquiry, and vote for a compulsory wind-up, in other words bankruptcy. They drew up a petition alleging that the management had been allowed to get into the hands of Alderman Galpin "who was not controlled by the directors", that the valuation of the assets had been carried out on a false basis and that secret mortgages were in existence purporting to override the debenture bonds. Then came the point which was all important to Walter Gray. They wanted to form a new company, composed mainly of the bondholders, to make a more economical realisation of the assets but first it was necessary "to secure the appointment of a skilled and independent liquidator, with whom we hope to associate a non-professional gentleman, of the highest standing in Oxford, whose name will at once command the bondholders' confidence."

As on so many occasions in Oxford's history, a determined effort was made to bring the power of the mob into play. A handbill was put out reading, "£100,000! Gone! Oxford Bubble Company!" announcing a mass meeting to "express public indignation at the reckless conduct of the Directors, Secretary and Auditors, who have caused total ruin to thousands and to express sympathy with the many widows and orphans rendered entirely destitute".

The authorities, instead of taking out a writ for libel or prosecuting the publishers for incitement to riot, went entirely on the defensive and prepared for a public explosion. The whole police force was ordered on duty and an army of Special Constables was enrolled. Before the mass meeting the effigy of an alderman in gown and cocked hat was drawn round the streets and after the meeting it became the object of a pitched battle between police and mob. The estimated size of the crowd was 6,000.

Perhaps there was something wrong with the company after all, for the authorities simply caved in. Messrs Galpin & Son, auctioneers and estate agents, went bankrupt, and Walter Gray, who was to go into the auction business himself, presided over the meeting of creditors. But what was more poignant was the case of poor Alderman Cavell whose name still adorns one of Oxford's most prominent shops. In those days wealthy tradesmen often lived over their premises which was convenient for business and other things too. One day, thinking that all was lost, Alderman Cavell went to the top floor over his shop and killed himself by jumping out of the window. Walter described him as "one of the best men who ever lived".

At this point Walter brought into play the social connections he had formed at Keble by getting Dr Talbot to write out a certificate attesting to his fitness as a liquidator. Why anybody should have accepted Dr Talbot as an authority on such a subject was never explained but, when the matter came up in the Chancery Court, the Judge announced that if anybody appeared to oppose the appointment of liquidator he might have to pay costs, in spite of which there was an objection from the liquidator nominated by the company, a Mr Fletcher. He said, in fact, that he was the liquidator since he had never been disowned by the shareholders. Walter was appointed by the Court, but Mr Fletcher gave notice of appeal and it looked as if nothing could be done until this was heard. There was now a consultation between the chief debenture holders and the directors of the company, some of whom were in favour of a truce, and ultimately it was agreed that, if the debenture holders abandoned their threats to have a thorough inquiry into the conduct of the board, they would accept Mr Gray and so he was appointed liquidator.

He got £600 a year which meant that he could go into business on his own account. He took possession of the Society's office and control of the staff, and he was in a position to form a new company. Moreover, he had won a great municipal battle and shown himself the most powerful man in Oxford.

Only one voice raised itself against the arrangement: in the Liberal *Chronicle* appeared three letters signed "Penny Wise and Pound Foolish", "Sold Again" and "A Betrayed Bondholder". The first referred to "an inexperienced Liquidator, whose recent relations with the Directors and position in Oxford quite forbid us to think that he can be independent, even if he desire it".

"Is it a fact", asked the second letter, "that the Steward of Keble College, Oxford, has been put forward by Mr Dayman to become Liquidator and dictator of this Company, and what is to become of the Company's property? Is it the fact that he is being backed up by a certain notorious clique for purposes half political, half personal? Is it the fact that he has actually had a friendly meeting with the Directors, whom it will be the duty of an independent liquidator to approach in quite another fashion, that he has shaken hands with them all round, and has actually secured their support, and upon what terms?"

What was the meaning, asked the third letter, of this "amicable coalition" between Mr Mallam, the solicitor for the bondholders, who had promised redress for his clients, and the directors? "In the recent communications from Mr Mallam", the writer continued, "not one word has been said about investigation nor the Oxford County Court, but we hear of a local man possessing a few shares in the Company, and with some experience as a college servant, proposing at Mr Mallam's instance to resign and become liquidator, of course for life, and this by arrangement with the Directors into whose conduct this puppet of theirs will, no doubt, honestly and strenuously inquire. Were retainers ever more abused, or bondholders more betrayed?"

Walter went to Mr Mallam's office, threw the newspaper on the desk and asked what the solicitor proposed to do, at which the solicitor wrote a letter to the editor of the newspaper demanding the names of the writers, under a threat of a libel action. The editor abandoned the fundamental rule of journalism to protect the anonymity of contributors and replied that Mr Robert Buckell had written all three.

Now this Robert Buckell was one of the younger Liberals, a coal-merchant who was working his way up in his party as Walter was in his. He claimed that he merely delivered the letters to the newspaper office, because the writers were afraid of being recognised, to which the editor replied by saying he even came back to correct the proofs. Walter decided to let it go, and indeed went out of his way to get to know Buckell.

Not the least remarkable fact about him was that, having won a tough battle, he worked just as hard to placate his enemies and promote that spirit of harmony which suited him so well so long as he was on top. It was with Bobby Buckell that he soon formed his most valuable alliance and, after the departure of the older generation, it was these two men who were to run Oxford for nearly forty years. Almost more remarkable, after all the bitterness, it was to a member of the Galpin family that Walter had his son articled.

He resigned from Keble, moved into a new house and set up as an auctioneer and estate agent to take the place of the Galpins, but gave this up before long and, when years later his son asked him why, he replied: "Why should I advise some fool how to make £5 when I could always make £100 for myself?" He was on the way to real wealth.

FRANK GRAY
CAVALIER OF THE COURTS

7

Local Giants

WALTER GRAY's son, Frank, was born in 1880 when the family still lived at Keble and he could remember until the end of his life the move to a private house in North Oxford, which signalised Walter's leap up the financial and social ladder. While still a child, Frank realised that there was one person his father was frightened of, his own mother, because whenever he had to visit her he made the boy go too. Thanks to the Building Society affair, Walter became a prominent man in Oxford and in almost no time he was mayor of the city, which meant a certain amount of publicity which he enjoyed. His mother knew all about his success and was proud of it but for some reason or other always complained about the expense. When she asked him how much a dinner had cost he never admitted the whole cost but this did not save him from the denunciation: "Fool". What was particularly galling to Walter was her insinuation that he had either defrauded her or was plotting to do so. On one occasion, when she was bedridden she had the small boy brought into her room, and then told a servant to fetch her silver and have it laid out. "You know," she said to Frank, "when you're lying in bed and it may be your death bed, and you have nobody but strangers about you, it's just as well to have a review of your belongings from time to time." The small boy to whom she said this realised that he was being made a witness against his own father. On another occasion, she said to

Frank, "I want you to have something to remember me by—a ring, a really good ring worth at least £50". Then, after a moment's thought, "You can get the money from your father: he has £600 of mine". He had actually lent the money to himself on a mortgage which was the best investment she could have had.

At 94 she had perfect hearing and eyesight, in fact, as they say, "all her faculties". A slight illness forced her to stay in bed for a few weeks, but this would have been of no importance if she had been satisfied to leave the household affairs to the girls in charge. But she thought they were idling away their time so she ordered them to move all the furniture on the ground floor from one room to another, making the sitting-room into the dining-room and vice versa. When they said this had been done she refused to believe them, struggled out of bed to see for herself, fell down the stairs and died.

Walter was determined to have his own son properly educated, as befitted his new status, and got him into Rugby where the headmaster was Dr Percival, who had been President of Trinity, Oxford, and was afterwards to be Bishop of Hereford when he shocked everybody by inviting the Nonconformists to share a Christmas Day service. Frank worshipped Dr Percival and started to learn Liberal ideas from him but he learned not much else and was, in fact, so backward that when he announced that he wanted to emigrate his form-master heartily agreed. But his father would not hear of it and had him sent to a crammer at Woodstock, Mr F. B. Harvey, who lived in the Dower House and punished refractory pupils by making them play billiards with him on a table in the barn until three in the morning. He wore an old silk hat and a long overcoat with the collar turned up even in the middle of summer and, in this garb, every Sunday morning he led his pupils to church in complete silence which was never broken until they were sitting down at lunch, when Mr Harvey would sigh deeply and say, "I wonder if you fellows realise what a sacrifice I make to set an example to you by listening to that old fool the Rector".

Frank had a story about another Woodstock character, the

Duke of Marlborough, who decided when he wanted to sell part of the Blenheim estate to act as his own auctioneer and took out the necessary licence. "As an auction," wrote Frank, "it cannot be deemed to have been a great success but as a rendezvous for the curious it exceeded all expectations." Apparently, the hall was crowded to suffocation and before the proceedings began a way had to be cleared for a procession of local auctioneers who formally if ironically presented a hammer to the Duke. This done, the Duke opened the proceedings by offering one small farm for sale. Now, at the front of the crowd was a well-known drunk, who was so delighted to be near a duke that he bowed happily whenever the noble auctioneer looked at him and the Duke took every bow to mean a new bid, with the result that the price went up to an astronomical height, to the growing astonishment of the Duke and the merriment of everybody else in the hall. At last the drunkard's attention was distracted and when he failed to bow the farm was knocked down to him. Suspicious at last the Duke required him to sign a contract on the spot, which he did, but on being asked for a deposit explained that he would send a cheque later and made off. The truth was now explained to the Duke and he wisely decided to end his career as an auctioneer without further ado.

Frank learned enough from Mr Harvey to get himself articled as a solicitor's clerk, though no doubt it was thanks to his father's influence. This was in 1898 when he was 18, and in the fifteen years since the Gray family left Keble College a tremendous change had been brought about in Oxford by its two rulers, Walter Gray who ran the dominant Tory Party and Robert Buckell who, having gone to the top in the Liberal Party, employed his considerable skill to suppress his followers whenever they tried to form themselves into an effective opposition. The two party leaders showed what they could do in 1894 when Mr Bickerton, who was not only Town Clerk but City Solicitor and Accountant, went for a holiday, took a swim and was drowned. Buckell and Gray decided to separate the offices which had to be filled, and to bestow the Town Clerkship on a man who was not only totally unqualified but actually disqualified since he was a paid agent of the Tory Party. This man's name was Richard Bacon.

Richard Bacon came from the poorest of homes, had little schooling, started work as an errand boy and managed after a time to get a job as an office boy to a solicitor. In those days Penny Readings at the Corn Exchange were a popular form of entertainment and Bacon became the most popular reciter, so much so that people flocked to hear him. He was equally successful in the Parliamentary Debating Society, which was organised on the same lines as the House of Commons and in which he was made Conservative Prime Minister. It was on the strength of his performance as a debater that, when the vacancy occurred for a local Tory agent, he was given the job and afterwards became the local secretary of the Primrose League. In these capacities he caught the eye of the Conservative Central Office in London and he was made one of their professional speakers, in other words a paid hack. Frank Gray, who was a powerful speaker himself, and was to sit in two parliaments, said that as "a pure orator" Richard Bacon was the greatest he ever heard. There was one occasion when he had to take the place of a famous politician at a great Tory demonstration. The meeting began with a series of distinguished speakers but they left the vast audience cold until Bacon got up and immediately, as Frank claimed, "lifted them to heights of enthusiasm and passion". The noble peer at whose seat the demonstration was being held showed his appreciation by tucking a ten pound note into Bacon's hand as he left the platform and the orator was not at all abashed by this evidence that he was nothing more than a hireling. On the contrary, he dashed off (as Frank said) "to settle a few pressing liabilities".

Years afterwards, when Richard Bacon had been called to the bar he met Lord Russell of Killowen who had taken an interest in his career and, after they had talked for some time, Lord Russell suggested a drink, to which Bacon replied that he was a total abstainer. "Good God," said Russell, "you are the only political hack I have ever met who could say that." But he had another vice, gambling, which never left him and he was in debt from the time he was 14. This, of course, was not known when the proposal was made to appoint him Town Clerk, though it is doubtful whether it would have made any difference.

The only people shocked by the appointment were some members of the University, which had only recently become entitled to nominate members of the City Council. These were chiefly the great law authorities, Sir William Anson and Professor Dicey. They decided not to make a fuss, however, but to have Bacon educated, and ultimately he was called to the Bar.

The Liberals accepted this extraordinary appointment because the other offices went to them, and in particular to Dr Harry Galpin, son of the unfortunate Alderman Galpin of the Building Society and a qualified solicitor. It was to him that Frank was articled and almost immediately he received a rough reminder that he was no longer at a public school but had come back to a much more unceremonious life. Soon after joining the firm he was called into his Chief's office and asked to carry a note of instructions to another solicitor. There was a third man in the room whom he knew well.

This was Mr George Rippon, an intimate friend of his father's. The Gray house had a long garden at the back which ran down to a wall dividing it from another garden, and down both the gardens a distinct path had been worn by the two owners, who preferred to confer at this spot rather than in a club or office. Mr Rippon, years before, after a time spent in America came back to England, settled in Oxford and bought a struggling weekly newspaper. He was up against a stronger Liberal paper as well as a Conservative rival, but Mr Rippon after sticking to the Liberal policy for a time suddenly switched to a Conservatism of such ferocity that respectable Conservatives felt bound to express their disapproval in public. Mr Rippon contributed a column under the name Jack O'Lantern in which week after week he lashed out above and below the belt scorning every threat of a libel action. In private the Tories began to hug themselves with glee and Mr Rippon's paper prospered, so much so that he was able to buy up his Tory rival and even threaten the Liberal *Chronicle*. His paper was the *Oxford Times*.

The reason why Gray and Rippon met surreptitiously was that they were in league, and no doubt much of the information with which Jack O'Lantern made so much play came from Walter. But on the meeting with Walter's son in the City solicitor's office Mr Rippon gave no sign of recognition. Much abashed Frank picked up the note which he had to deliver and went out in a leisurely way. He had not gone far along the street when he was seized by the scruff of the neck and thrown to the ground. His assailant was Mr Rippon, who shouted "Haven't you got a note to deliver? Why aren't you running?" The dishevelled young man said he didn't know there was any hurry. "There isn't," said Rippon, "but if you don't run everywhere you won't get anywhere."

This tiresome moralising had all too great an effect on the ex-public schoolboy, though he resented the indignity at the time, for he spent the rest of his life in far too much of a rush. But the sentiment would certainly have been shared by most of the characters who dominated Oxford life. Of course, there must have been a few citizens who stuck to a normal pace, or less, but they were the slow coaches who had no chance of reaching the top but, to judge by the men who most attracted Frank's attention, the place was in a perpetual whirl. One of the city's most celebrated sights was the famous surgeon Horatio Symonds, whose equipage was such as it careered down St Giles that visitors thought they were looking not at a doctor on his rounds but at a governor or pro-consul on some state occasion. Every morning at nine o'clock Frank would see the doctor in a half-brougham, victoria, or Irish jaunting car, according to the weather, with perfectly matched horses, small and lithe, chosen with care. The doctor's first call was at a florist's where a girl pinned an elaborate buttonhole to his lapel.

Mr Symonds had six pairs of horses and six coachmen, and the coachmen, all in fawn trousers and black coats, were chosen as carefully as the animals. He told Frank that once, when he advertised a vacancy in the local paper, there were 50 applicants and he invited them all to an interview at the surgery. The doctor asked only one question "How much beer do you drink in a day?" The first said none, the second a pint at supper, another two pints and so on. At last one man said a gallon, and the doctor said "You are engaged".

"You see, Gray," he explained, "I have a large country practice and in spite of all I say people give my men something to drink, so I need one who can stand it."

Once as his horses were in full cry towards a notice "Road closed" and the driver was starting to pull them up, the doctor stood up in the victoria and shouted "Drive on, man, drive on", but the horses slithered to a halt at a series of poles three feet from the ground, whereupon the eminent surgeon leaped to the ground, seized the poles and threw them aside one by one and then, to the amazement of the crowd which had collected, ordered his man to drive on over piles of stone and bricks and sand on the road which was being constructed. He reached his destination, according to Frank Gray, "shaken but triumphant".

Apparently the authorities took no action, but on another occasion he was even more headstrong. It was in the country and his carriage was careering towards a level crossing where the gates were shut. The doctor leaped out and shouted up at the signal box ordering the man to open them. When nothing happened he started throwing stones at the box with such effect that all the glass was smashed and the signalman had to take refuge on the floor. At last the law had to take notice but even now he escaped with a fine and apology.

The doctor was a great snob and threatened to leave his house merely because he heard that a retired grocer was moving next door. The same sort of snobbery affected the affairs of the Radcliffe Infirmary because the chief consultant physician, Dr Wingfield, was in his spare time chairman of a large grocery business. Dr Wingfield was as quiet and retiring as his colleague was aggressive and forceful. On one occasion, Symonds pushed past Dr Wingfield where a woman was lying, briefly examined her and turning to the house doctors, announced, "Operation at three this afternoon".

"But do you know what's wrong with the patient?" Dr Wingfield mildly asked.

"I said three o'clock this afternoon," said Symonds.

Dr Wingfield in his mild voice said that the illness had not been diagnosed and, even if an operation was necessary, why at three o'clock that afternoon? After which he electrified the audience by saying, "You know the public call you the butcher?"

"Do they," shouted Symonds, now beside himself with rage. "Well, they call you the bloody grocer."

He was a bully as well as a snob but his vices were outweighed in Frank Gray's eyes by the strength of his personality. What mattered was "courage and resource".

Another of the same breed was Judge Cook, famous for the strong language he used in court and determined to do justice as he saw it without bothering too much about formality. His most memorable exploit occurred in the sensational case against a certain Mr Pierce who, only three days after his own fashionable wedding, was charged with an act of indecency. Just before the hearing, the chief witness against him, a girl called Maud King, was arrested on a charge of stealing some boots from a shop, and the magistrates committed her to the quarter sessions. A difficult problem confronted the police who were certain of Pierce's guilt and determined to get him convicted. If Maud King were convicted she would have to appear at Pierce's trial in prison dress and this was certain to prejudice the jury against her. So Percival Walsh, who was Registrar of the County Court, consulted Judge Cook, Recorder of the Quarter Sessions, and argued that the conviction of Maud King, if it meant the acquittal of Pierce, would be a greater miscarriage than if the girl was let off. Judge Cook agreed and told the solicitor to make the girl plead guilty. Judge Cook's plan was to get the Mayor, who was chief magistrate, to make a strong plea for mercy on account of the girl's youth and previous character. In point of fact, it was the Mayor who had committed Miss King for trial but he agreed to fall in with Judge Cook's wishes.

However, when the girl appeared in court and pleaded guilty, the Mayor failed to recognise his cue and said nothing. Quite unabashed Judge Cook turned to the girl in the box and made the following speech: "King! It had been in my mind to pass

Men against the law: Frank Gray and W. R. Morris with pirate bus.

upon you a sentence of imprisonment, not merely as a punishment to you but as a deterrent to others. But, having listened to the eloquent and stirring appeal for mercy which has been made on your behalf by his worship the Mayor, I assume that he, as chief citizen and magistrate of this great city, must know more of the circumstances than myself and I bow to his judgement, only binding you over to come up for judgement if called upon." So Maud King duly appeared in ordinary dress as a witness against the young man, Pierce, who nevertheless was found not guilty thanks to the advocacy of Sir Charles Russell.

As for the Church the character most in the public eye was not the bishop or a college head, but the Vicar of Cowley, the Rev. George Moore (always known as the Reverend), and him Frank got to know well thanks to an equally dramatic character, the notorious Mrs Kingscote, daughter of Sir Drummond Wolff and wife of Colonel Kingscote, commandant of Cowley Barracks. She wrote successful novels under the name of Lucas Cleeve and Frank who had to serve a series of writs on her described her as the "finest adventuress I ever met". Whenever he called with a writ, she received him in her drawing-room and asked him to have a glass of port. She was middle-aged at the time and long afterwards he said, "I thought that this woman with the consuming brown eyes was the most wonderful thing on earth". Apparently a cool nerve went with a warm personality for he described one occasion when she took the latest writ and copied out the words, "Victoria, by the Grace of God, Queen Defender of the Faith . . .", as the opening words of her latest novel, which eventually appeared with the title, "What a Woman Will Do".

On another equally difficult occasion, when Mrs Kingscote was particularly hard pressed, she invited a well-known estate agent to advise her on the value of a country estate, met him with a coach and pair driven by a coachman in resplendent livery and attended by a gorgeous footman, and so charmed him as he surveyed the country scene that before leaving he pressed a loan of £500 upon her. What he did not know was that the turn-out was on hire and not paid for and, what was even more important,

Frank Gray on the road, 1925: trying to reach the lowest.

that the estate on which he gave his advice was not the property of his hostess at all but belonged to a complete stranger. Needless to say, when Mrs Kingscote went bankrupt the estate agent did not think it necessary to ask for his £500 back.

Mrs Kingscote's bankruptcy was for no less than £100,000 and it was found that most of the money had been guaranteed by a Liverpool money-lender. The reason why a money-lender had behaved so recklessly was that he had a daughter whom he wanted to place in respectable or if possible high society. In order to bring this about Mrs Kingscote offered to take the girl to the south of France and introduce her to "everybody who mattered"—provided the money-lender made the loan. He succumbed to the bait and lost his money.

It appeared that the money-lender had accepted a couple of local parsons as sureties and one of them was the Vicar of Cowley, the Rev. George Moore, who thanks to Mrs Kingscote went bankrupt.

"The Reverend", as everybody called Mr Moore, was a giant belonging to the same breed as Judge Cook and Symonds, a man used to getting his own way and not afraid of a little disturbance. The parish had an unsettled history and when the Reverend was instituted in 1875, the hope was publicly expressed that he would usher in an era of tranquillity, instead of which his 53 years as Vicar (he lived to be 86 and died in 1928) were of almost unbroken turmoil.

As a member of the local council he hardly ever attended without provoking a violent quarrel. He used the pulpit freely to get his own back and, as the *Oxford Times* said, "in his discourses he spared no one". The freedom of his language was highly popular, and such crowds wanted to hear him at the Harvest Festival that he spread it over two Sundays.

He farmed 600 acres and always had a couple of bob-tail sheep-dogs with him. He hunted and it was said, when his favourite mare died and he gave it up, that he had ridden eight hours a day for 25 years. His serious work was in starting a clothing and social club for the Cowley people and in getting schools built for the children. At a rummage sale a woman took his picture and said she was going to sell copies at sixpence a time. "You won't sell a dozen", said the Reverend, but she sold 273 at 6d. a time and one woman bought 14 to send to all her grown-up children who owed their education to him.

Mr Moore's most scandalous behaviour took place in his own churchyard, where he was heading a funeral procession, when he noticed that his orders about the position of the grave had been disregarded and it had been dug where he had specifically said it should not be dug. This had taken place because he had had a furious quarrel with his own sexton, who had turned up to see what would happen and was hiding behind a tree as the mourners advanced. When he saw his enemy, the Vicar abandoned the procession and, stopping only to get hold of a pick which was lying by the grave, rushed with a cry of rage at the sexton who leaped over a wall and made off over a ploughed field. Not at all deterred, the parson followed suit but, encumbered by his clerical garments, failed to overtake his quarry and soon gave up. The mourners had been watching in horror and were even more amazed when the Vicar returned muddy and breathless to complete the burial service as if nothing had happened. When an account of the affair appeared in the local Press, the Rev. George Moore began to be regarded somewhat askance, but the remarkable thing about this headstrong cleric was that the more outrageous his behaviour the more his parishioners loved him.

On one occasion he bought a set of harness at a sale but was accused by a dealer of taking home not the harness he had bought but a different set which belonged to the dealer. His accuser called at the vicarage to demand what he claimed to be his rights only to be thrown out by the Vicar, who then went upstairs and began to bombard the caller with everything he could lay his hands on. The dealer retreated to shelter behind a tree, found a spade and tried an occasional rush at the door but all to no purpose, only to be pelted with more and more missiles from above. This siege went on spasmodically for three days and attracted considerable crowds, but in the end the horse-dealer had to abandon the field.

It required more than a bankruptcy to distress the Vicar of Cowley, who had considerable experience of the courts in more alarming ways. He had his enemies in the parish as well as his admirers, and on one occasion felt himself called upon to issue a writ for slander. After a trial lasting three days the jury failed to agree and the judge ordered a new trial. At the first trial much turned upon what could or could not be seen through a keyhole. Before the second trial an eminent lawyer, whose services the Vicar had recruited, studied the evidence and then asked whether anybody had satisfied himself that there actually was a keyhole in the stated place. The Vicar's solicitor had to confess that nobody had bothered about this and, when the omission was rectified, it was discovered that there was in fact no keyhole. Thanks to this the Vicar's enemies were completely discredited at the second trial and he won damages and costs.

Even more publicity was attracted when proceedings were taken to have the Vicar unfrocked on the grounds of adultery. Mr Moore was 63 at the time and one of the accusations was made by a girl called Eustace who disappeared before the opening of the case and could not be found. Her allegations were dropped. The serious allegations were made by the Vicar's housekeeper, a Miss Johnson, who wrote to the Bishop claiming she had been seduced, fell on her knees afterwards to beg the clergyman's forgiveness but then thought better of it and renewed her allegations. The case before the consistory court started on a Wednesday and the rest of the week was entirely occupied by the prosecution, so that nothing of the defence had been heard when Sunday came. Mr Moore, who was a powerful preacher, let it be known that he was impatient to make his defence known and did not intend to wait for the court to resume but would answer his enemies in church. The result was that at eight o'clock on the Sunday a queue began to form outside the church and an hour later reinforcements of police were hurriedly called up to clear a way through the crowds. It is doubtful whether there has ever been such a congregation in an Oxfordshire village. Deafening applause greeted the Reverend when he came out of the vicarage, his white hair gleaming in the November light. By this time spectators had swarmed up the trees and people were clinging to the outside of the church walls in the hope of hearing through the ventilators.

The police had to force a way so that the Reverend could get to the pulpit and there at last he stood defiantly facing the world. His text was "Tell us, therefore, what thinkest thou, is it lawful to give tribute to Caesar?" and he started by saying that the Pharisees cared nothing for the answer but only wanted to catch Our Lord. There followed an unbridled attack on everybody who had given evidence against him in the court and, as the diatribe mounted, applause broke out and rose into wave after wave of cheers. Nor were the hallowed premises allowed to recover their habitual calm in the evening, when the Vicar roused even greater enthusiasm by preaching on the text, "I will not let thee go unless thou bless me"—popularly believed to be a reference to the disloyal servant.

In spite of this highly original method of giving evidence, the vicar lost the case and was found guilty of adultery, bad language and ribaldry. He was an undischarged bankrupt at the time, thanks to Mrs Kingscote, but somehow he managed to borrow enough money to take the case to the Court of Appeal and had the satisfaction of seeing the result quashed on the ground that the Consistory Court had acted solely on Miss Johnson's un-corroborated evidence. When he got back to Oxford, he found a crowd of admirers at the boundary of the Cowley parish. A brass band struck up in his honour. He was pulled from his carriage, hoisted on to shoulders and paraded behind the band and a torchlight procession.

Mr Moore, who always wore heavy checks and drove a spirited little pony, lived to be 86 and kept his popularity to the end despite, or perhaps because of, his irregularities.

8

Ceremonial matters

THESE were some of the figures who provided copy for
the Press and work for the lawyers. It was an unconventional
age and Frank's superiors, as he soon discovered, had a high old
time manipulating affairs to their own advantage. Frank used to
tell a story according to which he was acting in negotiations for
the sale of a fragment of land which the Corporation required
so that they could round off the pavement in one of Oxford's
main streets and the Town Clerk agreed to pay a sum equal to
the number of gold sovereigns which could be packed along the
side of the newly rounded pavement. The transaction was about
to be passed by the council when a newly elected representative
of the University, who was not yet well enough versed in the
Oxford way of doing things, made a speech which ran something as follows: "Your Worship, I am not rising to object to
the amount of money involved, excessive though it is. I am not
objecting to the method of deciding the amount, original though
it is. All I am pointing out is that this strip of land belongs to
the Corporation already." Possibly this was apocryphal but in
conveying an idea of the way things were done it is not
outrageous.

Frank found himself playing an important part in one of the
most important private "arrangements" because, whenever a
brewer wanted a licence for a new public-house, it was he who
was deputed to appear on behalf of his master, the City Solicitor,

to instruct the Town Clerk to apply for the licence, and the application was made to a bench of magistrates of which his own father was chairman. That it was possible for a City Solicitor and Town Clerk to apply for licences, as he used to say, "did not fall short of the amazing", but it appeared when the pantomime came under scrutiny that it was not the City Solicitor and Town Clerk who were involved but Messrs Galpin and Bacon in their capacities as solicitor and barrister. The device became so flagrant that it caused a public scandal. The Churches, the temperance movement, the brewers who were not being favoured and every grocer with an off-licence suddenly came together in opposition and it became obvious that the Oxford authorities might have gone too far, especially when it became known that one of their decisions was going to be challenged by a K.C. from Birmingham, Mr Vachell, who was known for his truculent manner and crossed eyes.

At the hearing before the magistrates, as soon as Bacon had started to speak, Mr Vachell intervened with the words, "Would the Town Clerk kindly elaborate what he has just said?" Red in the face, Richard Bacon protested that he was appearing not as Town Clerk but as a barrister and member of the Oxford circuit. Mr Vachell offered a suave apology, telling the Bench that it was a matter of considerable gratification to him, as he was sure it was to them, that Mr Bacon did not appear with all the advantages of his official position in Oxford but, like himself, only a humble member of the English Bar, anxious for no other advantage than that accorded by merit and actuated by no other feeling than to place before an impartial body the true facts upon which they could decide.

Mr Vachell must have known, as everybody else knew, that the Bench had already decided to grant the licence and was not concerned with the "true facts". But his job was to cause embarrassment in what he called "Oxford's happy family party", and this he successfully did throughout the day. Having made the Town Clerk squirm, he next turned to the other City Office which made possible these happy family arrangements, for Mr Bacon had not gone much further when his opponent said he was

87

surprised that the City Solicitor had instructed Mr Bacon to such an effect. This led to a blustering defence of Mr Galpin, by Bacon, to which Mr Vachell offered an even more elaborate apology in the course of which he said he only wanted to honour his old friend, Mr Galpin, and recognised the advantage he had in applying for a licence before his own Bench.

As the day wore on Mr Vachell became more and more eloquent in complimenting this Bench on the fame of their impartiality and more and more humble in referring to the grievous error committed by his own clients in having called in himself from outside the "family party". These speeches were peppered with the inadvertent use of the terms "Town Clerk" and "City Solicitor", which never failed to draw the inexperienced Bacon; and then in reply Mr Vachell would apologise for his slip, but finally defended himself by saying that he was speaking to his brief and the solicitors instructing him seemed to think that the only strength in the applicant's case rested on the appearance of the Town Clerk and City Solicitor before their personal friends on the Bench.

"We left the court dishevelled and discredited," said Frank with a guffaw. "The whole affair had been very unpleasant and, we thought, very uncalled for!"

After four years with Mr Galpin Frank had his articles transferred to London, to the Hon. Bob Lyttelton, Mrs Talbot's brother, an awe-inspiring figure who dressed in elaborate mid-Victorian style. According to the clerk from Oxford, his leader impressed the clientele less with his knowledge of the law than with his personality. On being handed a document, his chief concern was to see that his name was spelled correctly and his clerks breathed more freely when he had satisfied himself on this point for, if he was led by a mis-spelling to take an interest in the case, bad blood inevitably flowed and the dispute became less legal than personal. On one such occasion, a trifling point of disagreement developed into such a storm that the other solicitor threatened to go to law. Alarmed at last the Hon. Bob sent for his young clerk, handed him a letter and said, "What do you think he means to do?" "Issue a writ." "You're wrong there, my boy. He means to worry me to death." Having said which, the great lawyer reached for his hat, hurried from the office and went into hiding for a fortnight in the hope that the whole thing would blow over.

After a time Frank was entrusted with the job of drawing up the half-yearly report on a large estate and presenting the accounts, including Mr Lyttelton's costs. When he had finished his work, he would hand the documents to his chief who, without troubling to look at them, left for Carlton House Terrace, where the three trustees, all peers, invariably held a lunch party for the occasion. "Well," one of them would say, when the cigars had been lighted, "I suppose everything is in order, Bob. We can leave all that to you. Have you got any cheques for us to sign?"

This completed the business of the day and, when the solicitor returned to his office, he handed Frank the documents which had not even been opened, let alone examined. This delightful way of doing business came to an end, however, when one of the original trustees died and a Mr Oakley, brother-in-law of one of the beneficiaries under the will, was appointed. On the day of the next half-yearly meeting, Mr Lyttelton failed to return to the office at the usual hour of three in the afternoon and it was not until six that he put in an appearance, angry and dishevelled. "That fellow Oakley," he said, "read every word himself; read all the accounts and papers!"

"Well, they were all right, weren't they?"

"Yes. But they might easily have been all wrong. The fellow is not a gentleman."

Meanwhile, Frank regularly attended the Chancery Court and tried to make his voice heard in the Bear Garden. His first job, he learned, was to run his adversary to earth. This done, he had to hand the summons to a uniformed official and let it be known that the parties were ready to argue before the Master. Masters had their individual foibles which could not be ignored. For instance, Master Archibald, according to Frank, particularly disliked a lawyer who was so far carried away as to put a hand on top of the partition which separated them. Throughout the argument, Master Archibald seemed to be sound asleep but as soon as a hand appeared it was harpooned by his pen.

After the Master had announced his decision, the plaintiff's solicitor had to produce the summons at the order office, otherwise the action could not proceed. An experienced clerk, appearing for the defence, knowing he had lost would try to sweep up all the documents on the table including the summons and hurry away before his opponent realised what had happened. This was only one of the tricks which produced the intolerable delays of the Chancery Division.

Frank was also surprised to note the remarkable courtesy which obtained in this division when the bill of costs came before the Taxing Master who would go through the various items with some such remark as, "Instructions for briefs 50 guineas—what do you say to that?" turning to the solicitor for the trustees who, having put down a similar item in his bill of costs would say, "Well, Master, at first I proposed to object to that but I have since considered that the matter was a very complicated one and we could not reasonably oppose the charge". When a trivial item was reached, say 6s. 8d., the Master behaved as if he meant to pass it without comment, but one of the solicitors would bridle, object to the charge on principle and get it struck out after an angry argument. So the taxation proceeded, every large item winning unanimous approval and every small charge providing the subject of a fierce wrangle.

The amiable compliance of the Masters made it possible for a solicitor to charge for an attendance even if he had no representative there. Sometimes solicitors and their clerks appeared before a Master without knowing whom they were supposed to represent. One day an experienced Chancery Clerk giving Frank his instructions for the day said, "There are two cases you have to attend before Master Binn Smith. They have been going on for 40 years. Some of the parties have died and their executors have died and other people have sold their interests. I will give you a list of all the parties and the firms representing them. It may be asked for and you will be the only one who knows."

He was the only one. At this the Master remarked, "Evidently this is an important matter, requiring lengthy consideration. I shall adjourn the hearing and, in the meantime, mark each of you gentlemen 13s. 4d. for your attendance."

In contrast with this easygoing old gentleman, Master Hawkins had a caustic tongue and, when Frank dared to quote an opinion barked, "Young man, don't quote counsel to me. Wearing a pound and a half of horse-hair on your head doesn't give a man brains", and again, "Has it ever occurred to you, young man, that 50 per cent of counsel must be wrong all the time; otherwise the courts would be closed".

With which sceptical note in his ear, Frank decided to go back to Oxford and set up on his own.

He was only 26 when he made this decision but of course he had great advantages. At the Oxford court his father was in the chair and most of the men on the Bench were his personal friends, while in every court in the neighbourhood there was always one friend on the Bench. "I hope justice was done", he would laugh but he came to think all the magistrates ought to be stipendiaries. Many of the clerks were as ignorant of the law as the magistrates themselves; while there was often not the slightest pretence that justice was impartial. This was particularly true of poaching cases which were usually judged by the men who thought they had been robbed. In one such case a magistrate showed remarkable delicacy by saying at the beginning, "This is my case, so I won't sit", but instead of retiring from court buried himself in the *Morning Post* from behind which came the remark, "It's a very bad case; what's the most we can give him, Gray?"

In Oxford, Frank had a particular advantage because he was a friend of the Chief Constable, who would let him know the prosecution's plans in advance so that, when the Bench seemed likely to be hostile, he could apply for an adjournment and wait for a more favourable occasion. The Chief Constable collaborated in another way. Despite their fright over the drink licence, the brewers still manipulated the law, this time through the Licensing Act of 1903, which was hailed as a blow for temperance but in point of fact could be a valuable weapon to any brewery anxious to get rid of an unprofitable house.

The "ceremonial", as Frank called it, was as follows. The Chief Constable would agree to attack an area in which the brewery wanted to get rid of a public-house and all the houses in the neighbourhood would be scheduled so that the Chief Constable, by comparing barrelage, would be able to prove that there was redundancy. Frank's partner would appear before the magistrates to pretend he wanted to save the licence against the police. The licence was always lost and then came the question of compensation. Frank would work out the amount of compensation, divide it between the various interests—freeholders, licensers and licensees—and submit the figures to a valuer appointed because he was a personal friend of the Chairman of Magistrates and would get something out of the transaction. The valuer, in London, would glance at the figures and say, "Have you worked them out as before?" and, on being told that he had, say "I'll cut them down 10 per cent as last year. Let's go and have a bit of lunch". So the figures were agreed, the matter was carried through and, as Frank chortled, "good business was done in a very pleasant manner".

"All went well," he said, "until we got more daring. We caused a hotel to be scheduled and referred for compensation. The house, converted into shops, was far more valuable than before, but this did not deter us from putting in a very large claim for compensation, based upon loss of barrelage, cost of conversion and the assumption that premises must be worth less when they were unlicensed than when they were licensed. The very amount of compensation and the fact that the magistrates were interested parties almost brought about our undoing. An inquiry was threatened, and incidentally we learned that every case before had been dealt with on an erroneous basis. For a time the affair was quite unpleasant, but it passed through with nothing more serious happening than a reduction of compensation in this particular case."

One of Frank's first jobs at a fee of one guinea was offered to him by William Margetts, manager of the Quaker firm of Oxford bankers, Gilletts, later to be merged with Barclays. Mr Margetts preserved the manners of his early Victorian youth and business with him was conducted with ceremony. When Frank called on him to discuss a business deal he would be met by the old bank manager with the words, "Pray walk in, my good sir", and he would bow the far younger man to the best chair after which he would bow even lower and say, "Now, my good sir, which will you partake of, a little port or a little sherry wine?" Then the decanters would be produced on a silver tray with a plate of biscuits. Mr Margetts would no more have thought of dispensing with this preliminary ceremony than of leaving his bank unlocked at night.

William Margetts was famous because of the risks he took. It was said that, one night, long after banking hours, he was leaving the building when a young parson came up to him, asked whether this was a bank and then produced a cheque for 37 pounds which he wanted to cash. The cheque was drawn on a London branch of the London and County Bank (later the Westminster) to which Mr Margetts might have referred the stranger. Instead of doing this, or taking some elementary precaution, Mr Margetts simply said, "How did you want it, sir, in notes or coin? Pray come in", and leading the way into the building opened the strong room and cashed the cheque. Three months later the same young man arrived at the bank, asked for the manager and was shown into Mr Margetts' room. He made no reference to the previous meeting and gave no sign that he knew Mr Margetts. He had been appointed curate at an Oxford church, and would be paid only £150 a year. Could he have a bank account? It was opened and his stipend remained the same for two years. Then he was moved to a rich living in London but his bank account stayed with Gilletts in Oxford. Seven years later he inherited a baronetcy and large estates in East Anglia, but he remained faithful to Mr Margetts until his death. Thus William Margetts built up an important business not through attention to the ledger but through personal judgement and unshakable nerve. From these qualities Frank was to benefit at the outset of his career, for he had a chance to do a business deal if he could raise £10,000 quickly and got it from the old banker without security. The deal had the advantage not only of making a profit but of showing that he could act independently of his father.

Frank acted for Mr Margetts in a case which startled the whole neighbourhood because nobody had dreamed that he could even be suspected of a misdemeanour. The case started with a shooting party held on a September day on land adjoining that owned by William Evetts, in his day a well-known cricketer, who afterwards wrote to the four members of the party accusing them of "wilfully maiming pheasants in September", i.e. in the close season. Nobody disputed that some of Squire Evetts' birds were found with broken legs on the day in question, but the sportsmen indignantly denied responsibility and, because each letter mentioned the other members of the party, which amounted to "publication", they brought an action for libel. Passions ran high, expensive barristers were retained and the costs began to run up to absurd proportions. But what focused public attention and attracted widespread publicity was the appearance of Mr William Margetts.

Frank always emphasised that the most important incidents so far as the verdict and damages were concerned had no material bearing on the truth, which was in fact never discovered, but showed the uncertainty of the law and the wisdom of evading its clutches. Apparently there had been a tenant of Squire Evetts, a Mr Shepherd, who had given up his farm that Michaelmas and had become very hostile to his landlord. Before deciding to launch the action on behalf of the shooting party, Frank went to see Mr Shepherd, discovered that he had a grievance against Evetts, got his promise to give evidence for the plaintiffs and took a statement, or proof as it is called, of his evidence.

On the afternoon of the first day after the trial had opened, Counsel for the defendant, the Hon. E. Coventry, said he thought it right to bring to the notice of the court the fact that Mr Gray had taken advantage of the adjournment to entertain Mr Shepherd to lunch although Mr Shepherd had been subpoenaed by the defence. The prosecuting counsel immediately explained that, although a subpoena had been served on Mr Shepherd by the defence, he had in fact made a statement of his evidence to Mr Gray long before this, whereupon the judge sternly told Mr Coventry that he should make certain of his facts before making such an accusation in open court; the prosecuting counsel heaped coals of fire on his adversary's head by informing the jury that he was surprised the learned counsel on the other side should have made an attack of this nature on a man of Mr Frank Gray's standing, and was equally surprised that the learned counsel should have thought that his chief witness could be bought with a half-crown lunch. From this moment, Frank chortled, it hardly mattered about the evidence, for the jury lost no opportunity of showing hostility to Mr Coventry.

The trial was by a judge and special jury. The solicitors had the right to get a list of the 30 special jurors who had been summoned and from whom 12 would be chosen by ballot. Apparently the defending solicitor did not bother about this, but Frank did and got his clients to go through it to see if there was any possible enemy among the jurors. On the contrary, Mr Margetts pointed out that one of the special jurors was one of his own subordinates, a Mr Day, who managed one of the bank's branches. Frank now had to make a decision: he could reject a juror without giving a reason, or Mr Day could be advised to tell the judge of his association with Mr Margetts, or the other side could be told of this strange coincidence and invited to object to this particular juror. Frank decided to do nothing. After all, the odds were against Mr Day's being chosen, and if he were it would be fun to see what happened.

When the ballot was held the first name to be chosen was Charles Day who then took his seat in the jury box and was promptly made foreman. Needless to say the case went against poor Squire Evetts, who could hardly have had circumstances more vilely against him and had to pay heavy damages and costs. However, Frank always thought the defendant and his advisers deserved no sympathy because of their complete misunderstanding of the local situation. Indeed, a friend of his afterwards went up to the Hon. E. Coventry and said, "What a fool you were to let your man defend the case". "Why?" said the distinguished barrister, "He had quite a good case." "What had that to do with it?" said the friend. "You would never get a jury in the whole county to bring in a verdict against dear old Billy Margetts." Personal reputation meant more than the law.

9

"Plenty of Push"

FRANK's reputation grew not only because of his influential connections and quickness of wit but because of his capacity for making friends and inspiring trust. He was no dry-as-dust lawyer and the drudgery of a job always bored him. He was a sort of personal relations expert, at his best in strictly human problems, the disentangling of relationships and the pacification of odd, even dangerous, characters. Everybody, or nearly everybody paid tribute to him and repeated stories of his success, getting vicarious pleasure from it. They regarded him as a public benefactor, but clever and amusing, a cavalier of the courts. Valuable clients were recommended to him by policemen on point duty. One man came to Oxford from over 20 miles away, went into a shop to buy a hat, asked the assistant to recommend a lawyer and got the inevitable suggestion. One woman came to him to ask him to sue for breach of promise and, when he asked why she chose him, she pointed to one of the most passionate letters in which the erring lover wrote, "Young Gray has plenty of push and will go a long way". This was an extraordinary stroke of luck for the writer, for the recommended lawyer instead of trying to get the biggest damages brought the couple together and the last scene so far as he was concerned was what he called a "solemn meeting at his office" during which all the letters were solemnly burned. The fact that this couple lived together happily for many years gave him intense pleasure.

Perhaps the greatest factor in his success was that, as the son of a rich father, he was not thought to be interested in costs and fees but in reconciliation and a sensible solution.

The only breach of promise case in which he connived at a total rupture was one in which he was a mere accessory. This concerned a young titled Scotsman of great wealth who, while up at Oxford, fell in love with a girl in a cake shop and wrote to his mother to announce his engagement which brought her rushing to Oxford in a state of alarm. The Dean of her son's college recommended her to see Frank Gray, which she did. The purpose of the visit, he soon discovered, was not to seek advice but to announce her intentions, which he said he approved without reservation, "and indeed with applause".

What he applauded was a plan to show not disapproval of the engagement but gushing enthusiasm. The determined mother had come to Oxford not with any desire to deflect James from his purpose but rather to encourage him and hurry things up. She wanted to see Dorothy at once. They must all dine together that evening and Dorothy must give notice next day. James's friends must all meet Dorothy and she must spend the whole of the Long Vacation at the ancestral castle in Scotland. When the nervous creature arrived there she found herself forced into a round of parties, tennis, golf, and stalking. Lady X put all her energies into the organisation of the programme, and the result was that at the end of the Long Vacation both James and Dorothy had had enough of each other, and the parting was by mutual consent. Lady X wrote to Frank to report the success of her plan. Frank wrote back a letter of congratulation. He received a curt note in reply enclosing a guinea which must have been, he said, to pay him for being the only person present at the rehearsal.

In another case Frank acted unprofessionally, and it was not the only time. A woman came to see him and said that her brother, a middle-aged man known to the public, intended to marry a young girl but had just received a writ for the breach of his promise to marry a girl "beneath him". The bridegroom was deeply in love with the bride, refused to tell her about the writ but also refused to go ahead while this remained a guilty secret, and both he and his sister thought there might be a nasty scene in church. This was certainly the eleventh hour, since the wedding was announced for next day.

They wanted it settled quietly at any cost, but Frank thought this was impossible when he learned the name of the solicitor on the other side. This man would settle nothing until a long bill of costs had been run up and, Frank said, perhaps not even then; he seemed to like the idea of costs even when it was against his own interest.

The bridegroom's sister suggested that he, Frank, should go straight to the girl and pooh-poohed his objection on the ground of professional etiquette. He seems to have been less bothered by etiquette than by the certainty of failure. This is what he said to her, "This is not the case to try such an experiment for it will fail directly I go to the girl. Faced by a man she will either refer me to her solicitor or take me to her mother or father, even if I get her alone to start with, and they will probably say the same thing and I shall simply be found out by the solicitor on the other side and there will be no settlement." He then said, "I can't go to the girl, but you can".

Frank gave his client certain instructions. First, she must learn a form of receipt so that she could suggest it naturally and get the plaintiff to sign. He coached her in the form of words so that she was word perfect. He recommended her to call on the girl and, instead of trying to see her without her parents, she was to insist on their being present. This was because they might be more interested in money than the girl. This proved to be so, and the girl under her parents' influence accepted a sum of money far less than the bridegroom was prepared to pay. What was most important, perhaps, was that Frank's part was never suspected, thanks to the coolness of the bridegroom's sister.

But he took an even greater risk because of this success. An old client, who had quarrelled with his partner, went to the same solicitor who loved a good bill of costs, which made it look as if all the partnership assets would be swallowed up. Frank advised his client to swallow his pride, go to his partner and say he would agree to a settlement to prevent everything going to the lawyers.

Frank tried to coach him in the form of receipt but the old man's memory failed him and he brought out of his pocket the bit of paper on which he had written down the words. His partner signed the receipt but reported this incriminating detail to his solicitor who stormed into Frank's office accusing him of unprofessional conduct. "Fortunately for me," said Frank, "he lacked proof."

The fact that he would go to great lengths to help people became more and more widely known and was responsible for bringing him some remarkable clients, who usually brought more trouble than reward. One of the most remarkable was a man called Noble, who arrived at his office unannounced one hot July afternoon, a middle-aged man, with a black beard and piercing almost black eyes. He came from another part of the country and had lived most of his life in France and Italy, but had recently bought a country house eight miles from Oxford.

This Noble wanted a will drawn up. He was anxious to leave the whole of his estate to a young Frenchman who was living with him and he was also anxious to leave his body to Oxford University for laboratory purposes. He wanted to make the Public Trustee his sole executor, and this only a few days after the Public Trustee's office had come into effect. In fact, he managed to create the grisly impression that it was thanks to the creation of this office that he was now free to leave his body to an Oxford laboratory. A week later he called to sign the will, did so and insisted on paying the lawyer's charge at once—always a wise proceeding with a lawyer, as Frank commented. Frank went home to dinner and soon afterwards received a telegram reading, "Come Noble tragedy".

Frank left for the country and afterwards wrote an account of what followed which puts him into the category of atmospheric crime writers:

"It was a sultry July evening and it was still light as I passed through a large village before reaching my destination. Little knots of men foregathered in the main thoroughfare, at cottage doors in earnest conversation and of one of these groups I inquired the way to Mr Noble. 'He is dead', came the first reply, before I was told that his house was beyond the next small village. The directions led me to a lone Elizabethan house—a manor house—guarded and secluded by a high, grey stone wall and a close boarded heavy gate. Only one side of the gate opened, for the hinges of the other side were broken. On one gate still remained a faded auctioneer's bill telling of an abortive sale three years ago. None were concerned to remove it or repair the gates. The whole aspect savoured of the Court of Chancery.

"On pushing open the gate to enter, I fell headlong over a retriever puppy and with the fall went my remaining nerve. To the left of the front door, a gloomy light fell from a window to relieve an otherwise dark house. The front door was ajar and I entered and made for the direction of the only light. It was a sparsely furnished room; it might have been the dining-room. The light came from a single candle set in a saucer in the centre of a table. On either side, looking at the candle, sat a youth and a middle-aged man, who had the appearance of being a farm labourer. As I entered the latter rose uneasily, cap in hand, and said 'I've been bearing the young man company till you came, now I'll be going'. I arrested his departure by a shower of questions, directed solely to him. I learned that the youth could scarcely speak a word of English. 'What has happened?' I asked. 'He's shot himself, he's up there', pointing above to a dark glistening patch upon the ceiling. 'When did it happen?' 'About three hours ago, when this young man came back with the milk from the farm.' 'Has the doctor been?' 'Yes, and nobody has been upstairs since and this young man wants something fetched from the bedroom beyond.' 'Have the police been?' 'No.' 'Have they been sent for?' 'Yes.' 'Who lives in this house?' 'Only him and this young man.' 'Is there any woman in the village who will come and sleep here tonight and look after this boy?' 'Nobody will ever come into this house, it's fair haunted; he was an anarchist and nobody ever came near the place.'

"The man then shambled out nervously, twisting his cap. I followed him into the village and got into conversation with the groups of villagers still gathered in the darkness at a respectful distance from the house. With difficulty I persuaded a man and his wife to take the French boy into their cottage. No one could be persuaded to go into the house, either in the darkness or in the light of the following day. It was clear that strangers would have to be imported to do any domestic acts in the house.

"I returned to the house to await alone the long expected arrival of the police. At midnight the local policeman of the old school arrived, very drunk, too drunk to explain the situation to and almost too drunk to be got, with the aid of the chauffeur, into the car to be taken to his home. In getting out of the car he fell flat on the ground and there remained for I, now worn out and unnerved and angry, told the chauffeur to drive on and I was led into expressing the hope that the next car would run over him.

"However, this hope was not fulfilled, for the next morning he met me at the scene of the tragedy with his inspector, looking very well, fresh and alert for business. The dead Noble was lying under a window with the hot sun streaming in, clasping a revolver in the right hand, and an open razor lying on a bed at hand, lest the revolver should have failed in its ghastly work. It was clearly a case of suicide and the police gave orders that the body was not to be touched till the jury had inspected it and the inquest was to be held the following day.

"In the meantime, I got into touch with the local undertaker and asked for the head man, who was well known for his complete efficiency in the conduct of funerals and was well qualified to take charge of the exceptional and peculiar funeral that was to follow the inquest. I asked over the telephone if Mr Siggars could come to my office. The reply was 'I'm afraid he can't.' 'Why,' I asked, 'Is he away?' 'No, he died last night, he committed suicide.' This tragic coincidence added to my difficulties but not nearly so much as did the incompetent, and inexperienced old gentleman who was sent to act as deputy undertaker, and who was completely unnerved and overcome by the joint effect of being called upon to act as undertaker for his late friend and also in so peculiar a case as I presented for his attention.

"The inquest opened dramatically, with the production of a letter, by the police, found near the dead body of Noble and purporting to be written by him. It stated 'I die by my own hand but murdered as surely as if the Jesuit Wilson had pulled the trigger'. The reference was to the Parish Priest, who had never had any communication with the deceased whatsoever.

"The jury took no time to find a verdict of suicide, while temporarily insane, the latter a true but unnecessary addition as there was to be no burial.

"The inquest over, it remained to prepare the body for the coffin for its removal late at night to Oxford University. The undertaker agitated and anxious had brought no assistant with him; no one in the village would assist to lay the body out and so I appealed to the police inspector and asked whether his constable would assist; he replied 'certainly', but after speaking to the constable, he said he was not prepared to assist and, added the inspector, 'It's not a job I can order him to do'. Indeed the job had become a particularly unpleasant one for the body had been exposed in hot July weather to the sun of two days.

"I felt I was in a difficulty so I walked along the main road to the local public-house to get a cup of tea. As I walked, I met two tramps. Inspiration at once came to me and I addressed them. 'Look here, you fellows, are you prepared to do a nasty job of work for ten shillings apiece?' They did not pause either to think or inquire the nature of the job, for they both spontaneously said 'Yes' and I realised that for a pound apiece I had been sent two men who would have committed murder. I said, 'Well, stay here and I'll send somebody to you who will show you what has to be done.'

"I took the undertaker to them and said 'Here you are, this gentleman will explain what has to be done.' I called the undertaker aside and said 'Now go and buy a bottle of brandy and a glass and if they look at all like giving up give them a good draught.' This scheme proved successful and after a cup of tea, I applied myself to my legitimate job which was to find and inspect every document to be found in the house to shed light on the estate and state of affairs of the deceased.

"Hour after hour I sat in the haunted house, till the day waned, twilight followed to be succeeded by darkness, and there I sat reading the documents and papers till came the light. And then

I came upon a vast collection of strange and forbidding photographs, but in these photographs lay the secret of the dead man's mentality; they explained his mode of life, accounted for his associate, made the method of his death explainable and established his insanity. I took possession of the photographs, as was my duty. And now the hearse wheels on the gravel broke the dead silence of the lonely, deserted house and I started to follow in the last journey of Noble, under the shadow of darkness not to a burial place but to an Oxford laboratory.

"The Will was challenged by relatives and the sanity of Noble at the time of making the Will became the issue, and in this issue the existence of the photographs became vital. Was it my duty to disclose them? I did not and the French boy won his case.

"And the boy? Well, he squandered the fortune and then drove a London General Omnibus!"

Although he regarded the drawing up of wills and winding up of estates as the drudgery business which provided a living for the dullest provincial solicitors, it also provided him with some of his most satisfactory experiences. On one occasion he took over from some executors a small solicitor's business and with it a "dear old gentleman", the managing clerk, John Long by name, who was very nervous and retiring. Mr Long was in a highly nervous state because one of his late master's clients had named him as executor. The dead man was called Charles Bossom and he had distinguished himself by having a family of ten and naming the youngest, with John Long, as executor of his will.

The Bossoms belong to the history of Oxford and this is how Frank described the patriarch: "Up to the time of his death, just before the first world war, he was never seen outside his home unless clad in a white smock, pleated at the chest, a garb to be associated with agricultural workers of the past. He was a masterman with a small haulage business and a business of river work. He had a wharf together with a small cottage in the heart of the worst slums of the city. He died at the age of 86 and left property of such value that after bearing all death duties, expenses, etc., each of his ten children would receive a sum in excess of a thousand pounds." Because the heirs were intensely jealous of one another, Frank used to describe how each one came to his office complaining and how he told each one to keep a careful note of what the youngest did, the whole story culminating in a scene at his office when he had the fire stoked up and had prepared huge dishes of buttered crumpets which so melted the complainants that they forgot all about their grievances and each gladly accepted his or her share of the estate. What pleased Frank most was that he felt he had overcome an unpleasant situation and faithfully carried out the wishes of Charles Bossom.

There was a much respected churchwarden of the parish in which he had his office, a Mr Frank Burden, and when he needed legal assistance he would consult Frank. One day Mr Burden asked Frank to see an elderly spinster who had recently come to live in the parish. He wrote:

"I found that this new client lived in mean lodgings, over a small butcher's shop near the slums and she only claimed as her own a small, ill-furnished sitting-room. She was lying in bed when I called to see her, and after the exchange of greetings and courtesies between us, she said, 'I want to give you something,' and with eyes blazing with excitement she put her hand under the mattress, produced a packet and handed it to me saying, 'Look at it. See what is there.' The packet contained Bank of England notes, large and small, to the value of £23,000. 'I want you to take that', she said, 'and keep it for me'. I replied that I would take it to the Bank and place it upon deposit. 'Oh no,' she replied, 'I don't want that. I want you to keep it exactly as it is.' I explained that there was certainly a strong room at my offices used for Deeds, but it was most unusual, and indeed unwise, to use it for money for any length of time. However, she pressed her point and I reluctantly assented. It was curious that she should have preferred a stranger (for that I was) to a bank! This strange financial instruction given to me, my client proceeded to give me instructions for the preparation of her Will. It was simple, if peculiar. I, whom she never had seen before, was to be the sole executor and the estate was to be divided, after payment of expenses and duties, into ten equal parts and so divided between ten missionary societies. So little did my client know about these societies she proposed so to benefit that I had a difficulty, even by reference to directories, to get the full accurate names and even addresses. My client anticipated an early death and insisted that her Will should be completed the same day. This I did and later called to see the old lady, with some grapes, accompanied by a clerk to act as a second witness.

"Two days later, I received an urgent message to call upon the old lady. I did so. When I arrived at the bedside, she said immediately, almost fiercely, 'I want that money back I gave you'. 'All right,' I said, 'I will go and get it.' I left feeling like a naughty schoolboy. I returned and handed the packet of notes to her. She handled and fondled the packet and then said 'You can take it back again with you. I only wanted to see that you had kept it, as I told you to do.' I felt angry at the whole proceeding and told the old lady quite plainly that I was not prepared to run the risk of keeping this sum of money in a strong room in order to run backwards and forwards to show it to her and, if I took it back again, it would be on the clear understanding that I placed it in my Bank on deposit in her name. She cried but assented to the proposal, upon which I acted.

"After this I called daily, until her death seven days later, for a talk and to take a few flowers or a little fruit. The funeral took place at a Corporation Cemetery on a dull November afternoon. Around the grave gathered the clergyman, the official and experienced sexton, the undertaker, four bearers and myself, the sole mourner and the only one person who had known her, known her for ten days only.

"The old lady had resisted every advancement of mine to ascertain her origin, the existence of relatives or friends, or any fixed place of abode she had had. And so she went to her burial unknown and unmourned. The curt acknowledgements of the various missionary societies of their legacies concluded the transaction. I have never since heard of the matter and so to me remains the insoluble mystery of the old lady who journeyed to Oxford with her estate in mobile form to die."

There were occasions when his temper failed him and, on at least one, he assaulted a client.

This was a certain James Everell, known as a local "puck" at the time, which meant that his love of pets ran to eccentricity. He kept a cat and a goat and a remarkable number of parrots, which were all given the run of his garden. On a summer's evening he would go to his window and play a few bars on a violin at which the pets would set up what Frank, oddly enough, called their "accustomed and unaccustomed noises". Their owner called it "Everell's local band". The first meeting took place at an auction sale where Frank wanted to buy a certain property and said, "Three" at which Everell said, "Five." This was much more than it was worth but there was another anxious buyer who said, "Five thousand five hundred", at which Everell exclaimed: "I thought you were bidding in hundreds."

Everell was an enthusiastic litigant and Frank gave the following account of him:

"He arrived at the County Court with one of the largest deed boxes I have ever seen. This, with difficulty, was found floor space in the vicinity of the witness box. The deed box was apparently filled with papers relating to the case in hand, and, I imagine, many other cases. Everell was the defendant and all went well during the progress of the plaintiff's case for he was not much of a cross-examiner. Immediately the plaintiff's case had closed, Everell took up a position in the witness box to explain his case. This was entirely dependent on the production of a number of documents.

"Everell was a fat, short-necked man and exertion told heavily upon him. He regularly punctuated his long stay in the witness box by 'One minute, your honour, I have got a document to show you,' and before the Judge could protest, or notwithstanding the protest of the Judge, with amazing agility he was out of the witness box and down on his knees at the deed box looking for a single document among stacks of irrelevant documents. As the hunt for the missing documents became hotter, deeper would go the head of Mr Everell into his box, till scarcely more than his short legs could be seen. He looked like a spaniel at a rabbit's hole. However long each search lasted, Everell always emerged with the document required at the moment, but he emerged in a dishevelled condition so that it was impossible for him to continue his evidence for an appreciable time. In vain did the Judge urge him to get out all the documents required at once and in vain did he protest that it was the duty of litigants to prove their cases. Everell assented to the general principle but with a hurried 'One minute' he would disappear from the witness box for a further search on the ground. At last the Judge adjourned the case for Everell to get all his papers ready but the case was never heard again. Either the Judge or the Plaintiff's solicitor anonymously paid the amount into Court to save a further hearing."

The remarkable Mr Everell went to see Frank on a busy morning and, producing a bundle of deeds, asked for a modest loan. He returned on several subsequent mornings always choosing a time when Frank was likely to pay up in order to get rid of him. Some time later, it was reported that Everell had disappeared and Frank realised that he had advanced more than the deeds were worth. He decided to cut his losses and had the property sold for what it would fetch. About three years later, Everell turned up and, as if nothing had happened, asked what had happened to the property. On learning it had been sold he blandly said, "Ah, lawyers aren't very honest are they?" at which Frank sprang out of his chair, seized the fat man and shook him violently, shouting over and over again in his wrath, "Don't you know you robbed me? Don't you know you robbed me?"

Finishing the story, Frank said, "Everell just blinked at me and fortunately never took proceedings."

There was one encounter which severely tested his temper but in the end was to prove his extraordinary gift for forming a personal relationship in the most unlikely circumstances. One day his clerk announced that "a gentleman wished to see him but refused to give his name". In spite of this he agreed to break a rule, as a result of which there strode into the room a man of about sixty, over six feet tall and with a black pointed beard. He rushed up to Frank's desk as if about to strike him and shouted in an angry voice "I want to ask you a question," after which he said, "How much?" and without waiting for an answer threw three half-crowns on the desk with the words, "Will that do?" He then put an abstract point to the lawyer, who although he was furious at having his opinion bought "like a joint of meat" angrily gave the answer, at which the bearded man strode out of the room leaving Frank crestfallen. His pride was hurt because he had allowed himself to be bullied into giving an answer to an abstract proposition and that to a complete stranger who had managed to get away without revealing his identity. It was miserable consolation that he had received 10d. more than he was entitled to. A month later the client returned, as angry looking as ever, announced that he wanted to ask another question and added, "Same terms as last time", as he threw down the half-crowns. Oddly enough, Frank again answered. He seems to have been more amused than angry this time and wanted to know the explanation for the whole thing. Three months passed and the client reappeared, this time not to ask a question but to get a letter written and this meant disclosing his identity. He proved to be a distinguished civil servant, now retired. Not long afterwards, Frank was standing on the platform at Oxford station about to get into a train for Reading when the unceremonious civil servant rushed up to him, seized him by the shoulder and shouted "I want you. I've got some deeds for you." Frank shook himself free and said angrily, "I can't bother with you now. I have an engagement in Reading", but the old man laughed and said "Then you'll have to come to my house for them. You will come to dinner tomorrow night." Frank meekly went and this was the beginning of a surprisingly intimate friendship. The retired civil servant had a country house 25 miles from Oxford where he lived with his wife who looked on his violent behaviour with tolerant amusement and took up the simple attitude, all too uncommon in wives, that her husband could do no wrong. With them Frank spent more and more week-ends but if he missed seeing them for a time an invitation would arrive in the least expected way. Once Frank was standing on Didcot station when he heard his name shouted from a train standing two platforms away. There was the bearded client hanging out of a window. "Do you like grilled ham and broad beans?" "Yes." "Do you like strawberries and cream?" "Yes." "Come to my place on Saturday and you can have both." Apparently the crowd on the station loudly applauded and, as Frank said, "one facetious fellow asked if he could come too".

During the week-end the two men went for long walks together, the host always leading with enormous strides and Frank trotting afterwards, hard put to it to keep up. On one occasion the host suddenly turned round and looked Frank full in the face, and said, "I wish I had a son like you", after which he set off again faster than ever.

On Monday mornings the host called the guest at an unearthly hour, ran a bath for him, shouted out when it was ready and waited in the breakfast room striding up and down impatiently. When Frank said there was plenty of time, he said angrily, "Your office opens at nine o'clock and it's my job to see that you get there".

Such was this father-and-son relationship. When he recalled the remark about his being wanted "as a son" it was the only occasion when Frank recorded a moment of sentiment. More typical was the way he laughed it off: "As I drew his will in favour of distant relatives I certainly wished I had been one of them."

He never mentioned the man's name.

10

The Underworld

THEN there were the scamps and dubious characters who formed a sort of underworld to which Frank was proud to belong. With some of these characters, particularly those who lived by their wits and were unafraid of the law, he formed lasting friendships through which he was encouraged to think of himself as not wholly committed to respectable society.

The man he admired most was a chimney sweep called Bill Soden who amassed a fortune of £70,000 but to the end of his days drove the traditional sweep's cart with brush raised aloft like a flag staff. In this vehicle with the blackened owner by his side Frank sometimes drove himself, grinning broadly and graciously acknowledging cheers from the bystanders.

Frank always explained that his friend had not amassed his fortune by sweeping chimneys at half a crown a time but because this humble activity proved an excellent cover for more lucrative business deals since "respectable" people were hard put to it to believe that a mere sweep had the resources to raise a bid or put through an expensive transaction. Soden bred dogs, dealt in horses, ran a horse slaughterer's business and most important had a wide circle of dubious friends, including horse thieves, who could always be depended on to give him vital information.

What aroused Frank's most fervent admiration was the little sweep's success in besting the authorities when everything seemed to be against him.

The outstanding occasion was when thirty horses arrived at the Oxford railway station consigned to Soden and the railway company demanded payment of the freight charge before delivery, which Soden refused to pay on the ground that the terms of sale were delivery at Oxford and the seller must be looked to for payment. The company thereupon impounded the horses in a field to which the only reasonable access was a narrow lane which the railway police were set to guard in case Bill Soden tried any funny business. Soden's retort was to get together thirty quite different ponies on the other bank of the river which bordered the field and then, at dead of night, drive them through the water into the field which his new acquisitions occupied.

Next morning, Bill Soden appeared in the lane leading to the field and said to the detective on duty, "Some of my ponies have got into the field you're looking after" and, when the detective expressed disbelief, induced him to go to the gate to count the occupants. Soden proposed that the only thing to do was to open the gate and let the horses into the lane where they could be sorted out.

The detective agreed, which was his undoing because as soon as the gate was opened the ponies stampeded, and the detective was unable to identify a single animal, with the result that Soden claimed the whole lot as his and in the end drove them all away without paying a farthing. This was what Frank called a superb example of "courage and resource".

Apparently it was thanks to Bill Soden that Frank knew most of the Midland gypsies and in particular the Bucklands for whom he always acted when he was in practice. His instructions never came from the individual who was "in trouble" but from the head of the tribe who would lead a deputation of minor chiefs. The leader in those days was Jacob, an ancient with black hair down to his shoulders, and he would open every meeting with the words: "Good morning, your honour, one of our boys has got into a bit of trouble." On one occasion after a knifing affair, Frank appeared for the tribe at the hearing of no less than 17 cross summonses for assault. On another occasion, when one of the boys was accused of assaulting a girl, he chose 15 swarthy young men and paraded the whole lot in court, asking the wretched girl whether she could positively swear who was the culprit, which of course she failed to do and the case fell to the ground. The legal consultations invariably ended with the following dialogue:

Jacob Buckland: "What will your honour's expense be?"

F. G.: "Fifty pounds."

Jacob: "Your honour's hard. We haven't got it. The poor boy must be spoken for."

F. G.: "No fifty pounds, no defence. That's straight."

Jacob: "The money will be found if we have to tear the wheels off the vans."

Next day the deputation returned with fifty pounds all in silver, to be laboriously counted. This, however, was only during Jacob's lifetime, for he was succeeded by John Buckland, who had an extra pocket sewn into the front of his trousers and carried in it no less than two hundred pounds.

Then there was Bill Jeffries, a legendary figure to generations of undergraduates for his knowledge of horses and dogs; in the nineteen-thirties, he was still the commanding figure at local point-to-points and rural shows, standing six-feet-four and leaning on a shepherd's crook. He wore a cut-away coat over his breeches and his hat was one of those cut-down toppers such as Winston Churchill sported. In his younger days Bill Jeffries had a hair of golden curls and Frank described him as "a cherub gone to seed". At that time he hunted a great deal and at a meet would offer to race anybody for ten pounds a side, the runners to wear hunting boots. Because of his size and ponderousness, somebody usually took him on, but he always won.

Frank's first acquaintance with him was over a claim for £59 which, it was claimed by a restaurant manager, was the price of a lunch supplied to a coach for seven undergraduates and Bill. Bill claimed that the price was extortionate but it was upheld in court and the undergraduates had to pay. Bill was even more indignant when he was made bankrupt, but he managed to raise enough money from friends to carry the case first to the Divisional Court and then the Court of Appeal. At one stage of the proceedings, he said to the judge, "Two millionaires will guarantee that", to which the judge, with an assumed meekness, said "One will do, Mr Jeffries". Bill apparently enjoyed these long-drawn proceedings because he had an excuse to go to London by train, first-class of course, and lay a series of heavy bets on the legal proceedings.

At last these proceedings came to an end and Bill Jeffries had to face what appeared to be inevitable, the loss of his farm. Now he took to haunting the bars of the market town in which lived the bailiff whose duty it would be to take over the property, and whenever anybody was within earshot he would announce that he felt sorry for this man, who had never done him any harm. From this it was freely reported that any bailiff who dared to set foot on Bill's farm would do so at his own risk, and was unlikely to escape with his life. These threats had their effect, for the bailiff informed the authorities that he refused to act. Moreover, nobody could be found to act as bailiff's man and remain in possession for the necessary eight days. In the end the police had to find somebody whom Frank always referred to as a "desperado from Birmingham", to wit an out-of-work boxer, and this desperado from Birmingham knew enough about Bill Jeffries to stipulate that he would have to have a mate when he did the job.

In fact when the expedition set out to take possession of the farm it comprised the bailiff, his two men, a police sergeant and four constables all armed with revolvers. They arrived at the local station and made for the farm, on the way passing a cottage occupied by one of the farm hands which had just recently been connected with the farm by a telephone wire so that Bill Jeffries could be warned of their arrival. All seemed quiet on the farm but the expedition advanced with caution under the command of the sergeant who disposed his force in "open formation" and told them to take advantage of every bit of cover. Within a hundred yards of the house, a halt was called so that everybody could get his breath back. After a few minutes the sergeant leapt to his feet, flourished his revolver and called on the enemy to surrender. There was no reply, so the sergeant ordered his men to follow him and rushed towards the house. As he reached the door it sprang open and everybody poured into the hall as if in a knock-about film comedy. When they picked themselves up they saw that the door had been opened by Bill Jeffries himself. He was beaming with delight, asked them why they had been so long and then marching to another door, flung it open and revealed a huge table groaning under what used to be called a "lordly spread"—poultry, joints, legs, puddings, cheeses and wine, all the property of his creditors.

The bailiff, and his assistants, together with Bill Jeffries lost no further time but sat down together to eat and drink their fill, after which the bailiff and police left after many mutual expressions of goodwill. Next morning a villager who happened to be passing was astonished to see Bill Jeffries and the two bailiff's men all dressed in white shorts and sweaters running round the farm. It appeared that the boxer was a certain Willie Burgh, the other was his trainer; Bill had decided to give a hand with the boxer's preparation for a forthcoming contest and the farm proved so suitable for this purpose that at the end of the eight days the creditors, as Frank said, were faced not with one desperate man, but three. They let it be known that they were staying on the farm while there was a single bite to eat and defied the police to expel them. All the creditors could do was to ask the court to commit all three to prison for contempt of court. Before this came before the court, Jeffries sent a message to Frank asking him to defend him and then, leaving the two boxers behind to defend the farm against all comers, emerged himself and went to Cheltenham to meet his lawyer.

Frank wrote, "I was horrified at meeting Bill, for he was not a depressed man, ready in a spirit of contrition to express his apologies to the Court. On the contrary, he was accompanied by a considerable and extremely questionable crowd, comprised of bookmakers, their clerks, touts, grooms and cabbies. He himself was in an atmosphere of great elation and this had intoxicated his followers. They would hear of no apology and no plea of guilty, and mob-rule was to be the order of the day."

Frank led this mob into the dining-room of an hotel, mounted a chair, and made a speech the burden of which that he would refuse to go into court unless everybody promised to leave everything to him, without interference. After a good deal of wrangling, Bill Jeffries agreed with the following words: "All right, guvnor, you say what you like and when you've lost we will have a go."

News of the mob's temper must have reached the authorities for the County Court, to which the matter had been referred, was crowded with police, which only agitated the mob still further. Frank made a brief speech claiming that the whole thing was due to a misunderstanding, the first object being to save Jeffries from immediate arrest. He not only achieved this but Jeffries was given 21 days to comply with the order, a decision which was greated by the mob with a roar of "Tally Ho". The judge, according to Frank's version, "hastened from the Court— unduly I thought".

This was not the only occasion when Bill Jeffries appeared in court, for he was arrested some time later because when a bailiff went to his house a shot was aimed at him through the letter-box and narrowly missed. The bailiff was ready to swear that he saw a revolver through the letter box but there was nobody to prove that Jeffries was inside, so he was acquitted. "He was certainly not there soon after when the police carried out a raid, so", Frank used to say in his most laconic tone, "he must have been innocent."

These were men of spirit who aroused Frank's imagination, but others were a dismal disappointment because they failed to respond to his rescue work. One of them was the Oxford Town Clerk, Richard Bacon, who after his extraordinary appointment proved highly successful as an administrator but gambled more and more heavily until he was deeply in debt not only to local tradesmen but to national money-lenders. At one time he proposed to get himself out of difficulties by going into racing as an owner, for which purpose he joined up with a corn merchant, a builder and a commercial traveller. They bought a horse and re-named it Oxford, but the animal ran so badly in its first race it never appeared again.

One day Frank got a note from Bacon asking whether he could call at his house that night and the Town Clerk's first words were "Unless you can find £3,000 for me quickly, I am ruined —and there's a lot to come out". He then produced a list of creditors, whose bills actually came to £3,500. Frank named a local draper whose name did not appear, to which Bacon said he had only put the pressing creditors on the list. Frank then said that he had been consulted that very day by the managing director of the firm in question as to whether it was wise in the long run to issue a writ against the Town Clerk of Oxford. "Does that make it pressing?" Frank asked, and he went on to question Bacon in order to find out the real amount of his indebtedness, which proved to be over £10,000 and more than half of it to money-lenders.

It was a case after Frank's heart—a man dependent on him, the cleanliness of local government at stake and a completely free hand to use his own wits and personality. Next day, after clearing up more trivial affairs at his office, he set out to see the Earl of Jersey, then High Steward of the city, had lunch with him and came away with a cheque for £500 as a personal contribution towards the rescue of an Oxford official. Almost more important than the cheque in Frank's eyes was the complete absence of any reproach that things had been allowed to go as far as this. The next call was on Lord Valentia, a poor man, who provided an even warmer reception and wrote a cheque for £100 with the words, "You tell your friend, Bacon, I wish I could make it ten times the amount but I can't. My bankers will cash this but they might not if it was any more".

That was the one sort of reception. The other sort was provided by a noble peer who talked for two hours on the help he gave his poor relations and refused to give a penny on this occasion. Even worse was a rich local tradesman who a few weeks before had feasted the Town Clerk and arranged plenty of Press publicity for the event. This gentleman drove Frank into a frenzy not by refusing to contribute, though that was disappointing, but by lecturing Frank on the sin of indebtedness as if Frank was the culprit. However, within three days the Richard Bacon fund stood at £3,500 and this was enough to stave off the creditors who were issuing writs or threats on all sides.

Now came the business of dealing with the creditors. This was made possible only by the fact that during a sea voyage Frank had met a young solicitor who acted for most of the leading money-lenders and who now advised Frank to hold a meeting under the chairmanship of an accountant who did similar work. The result was a meeting in a London hotel at which Frank argued that his listeners had done well out of Bacon over the years, that Oxford would not want her Town Clerk to go bankrupt but that his friends were exhausted. The money-lenders accepted a moderate settlement.

The salvation of the erring Town Clerk was now in sight. Deferred payment was arranged with the local creditors, a trust deed was created, Mr Bacon made contributions himself and in due course, as Frank said, he "stood up a clean man owing nothing to any man". But Frank had merely bought time and in due course Bacon was to go bankrupt, thanks not only to debts but drugs. His examination was regarded by the Registrar as sadly unsatisfactory because he managed to arrange a "great destruction of papers"—a favourite Oxford occupation in times of danger.

There was one other character who failed to respond with complete satisfaction to Frank's rescue work, and that was a certain Harry Wild who had been foreman to old Mr Money, the man who built most of Walter Gray's houses. Wild was an excellent builder and looked forward to the day when he would own the firm, but unfortunately for him he got a job rebuilding some stables near Wantage and when he asked the trainer for a tip was advised to put his shirt on his namesake at Ascot. This horse was called Victor Wild, and, when it won the Hunt Cup, Harry Wild won £15,000. This made him think gambling a more attractive way of making a living than building houses, but his fortune turned, he lost more and more and then absconded while still having enough money to justify his overdraft.

Years later, when Frank met him in London and took him to lunch at the old Holborn Restaurant, Wild broke down and said it was his first proper meal for months. As a result of this meeting,

Frank took over his assets managed his affairs and put him in charge of a new building estate which was being developed. However, as time passed Wild gave signs of going off the rails again, so Frank wrote to him alleging he was not doing the job properly, to which he received the reply, "If I have to make the choice, I would rather be a tramp than your bloody slave".

Frank always claimed that this was the spirit he admired, though I doubted that many years later when I was forced to make much the same sort of remark myself.

FRANK GRAY
LEADER OF THE MASSES

11

W. R. Morris threatened
with arrest

FRANK might have gone on as a solicitor, enormously successful both in making money and gaining prestige; he might even have become a stalwart of his father's political party, entered Parliament as a Tory and have become in time a figure of the establishment. When I knew him the idea would have been laughed down, but at the time when his life took a decisive course his ideas may have been different. The decisive factor was his friendship with W. R. Morris, which led him to think that his destiny was as a leader of men or, as he would probably have laughed, an "inciter of the mob".

It all happened because of the trams. As late as 1912 the only means of public transport in Oxford was the horse-drawn tram, a vehicle which figures nostalgically in pre-1914 University reminiscences but which had become a subject of derision. For six years the Corporation had been brooding on the need for modernisation. It had promoted two Acts of Parliament. An option was given to the National Electric Construction Company but it was to expire in August 1912 and there were no electric trams in sight. The horse-tram workers went on strike (for sixpence a day) and Oxford then had no public transport at all.

The National Electric Company—of which, incidentally, Sir Robert Buckell was a director although he was chairman of the city Watch Committee—now brought forward a new proposal for a mixed electric and petrol system. This was accepted by the General Purposes Committee on condition that the Company paid a fine of £1,400, but there was public uproar. A meeting in the Town Hall broke up in disorder and Professor Dicey was one of those assaulted. Finally, the City Council threw out its own committee's recommendation and there was total deadlock.

At this point W. R. Morris, who ran a garage business and was best known as a racing cyclist, wrote to the Town Clerk of Oxford asking for a licence to run two public buses and got no reply. He consulted Frank. It was obvious that the Corporation could never grant a licence which would cut right across its contractual engagements and form a precedent, and so Frank decided that the only hope of success was to marshal public opinion and whip it up to the point where it would carry all before it; in other words, the mob was to rule. This may seem an exaggerated description of this crucial episode in the career of the man who was to become Lord Nuffield, but in Frank's account of the affair he takes full responsibility on himself and there can be no doubt that he was peculiarly fitted for this exercise in public leadership. In fact it was to prove an apprenticeship for his career as a politician, but it is doubtful if he knew in which direction he was going, "Like many other great battles", he wrote "this was determined by the course of events and our action was determined by the action of the enemy rather than any well thought out plan. . . . It is doubtful whether either of us would have had the courage to go on if we had foreseen all that was to happen."

The first decision was to defy the Corporation by putting a couple of buses on the streets without a licence, but these were to be buses with a difference because anybody who used them would not be able to pay the fare on the spot. Coupons could only be bought in advance and the public could get them either singly or in bulk at certain shops where the conniving tradesmen were given a 10 per cent commission. Frank claimed that this idea was entirely his but he could never explain precisely what was the point of the arrangement. In fact, it had no point since an illegally plying bus could hardly be made legal because the tickets were bought in a shop instead of on the vehicle. But it helped to "confuse the issue".

Advertisement space was bought in the local papers and the public was informed that the petrol-bus service would positively start on a certain day. On the fateful morning Frank gave a champagne breakfast for W. R. Morris and their chief supporters, after which the two men left for the place where the first bus was to start. They found a crowd of would-be passengers who alternately cheered the petrol bus and jeered an old-fashioned tram nearby drawn by a miserable horse.

Among the passengers who managed to get on the first bus was a police inspector, who conformed to the rules by producing a coupon, and a sergeant who offered 2d. to no avail. The bus started and went non-stop to the middle of the city because, being full, it had no need to stop at the various points where cheering crowds hailed it and tried to get on board. At the end of the journey the inspector jumped out and ran to the driver, whereupon Frank who had been in W. R. Morris's car behind the bus, followed him and interrupted the conversation in a way which, he afterwards admitted, betrayed his truculence, unreasonableness and nervousness. He said "Mr Morris and I are responsible for the running of this bus which we claim the right to do. The driver and conductor are strangers to Oxford and they have agreed so long as possible to remain at their posts, whatever may be the consequences. But Mr Morris and I take sole responsibility. This bus will continue to run, and any force used to stop it will be met by force." A melodramatic declaration which (Frank afterwards admitted) lost much of its force thanks to the dignity of the inspector, who quietly replied, "I hope nothing of the kind will be necessary, Mr Gray. I only have to make a report and I am making a note that you and Mr Morris take full responsibility for this breach of the law and anything which may result."

During the course of the day, the whole population of Oxford seemed to be trying to get on the buses. But then Frank received a private and personal note from the City Solicitor to whom he had been articled. This note informed him that there had been an emergency meeting of the Watch Committee as a result of which he, the City Solicitor, was instructed to apply for a warrant for the arrest of the drivers and conductors of the buses and of Mr W. R. Morris and Mr Frank Gray.

This must have been the most sentimental letter Frank ever received and the most difficult to ignore. Mr Galpin reminded Frank that he had been his favourite pupil, and that if he were forced to make this application for a warrant for his arrest it would be the most painful duty of his life. It must indeed have been an excruciating situation for the old man even to be brought to the point of having to consider such a decision. Mr Galpin ended by appealing to Frank to do something which would prevent such a painful conclusion.

Frank's reply was unsentimental: he was very sorry but all the consequences had been considered and the matter must take its course. Frank wrote afterwards: "The matter had now assumed a very grave position, for within 24 hours our drivers and conductors were likely to be arrested and ourselves to boot."

In an effort to prove that the public was on their side the law-breakers decided to call a public meeting as an alternative to surrender, but they realised that a bad meeting would be worse than nothing at all and the only way to be certain of success was to hold the meeting at once while the public was excited. But how could they get the advertisements out in time? There was a local printer, one Joseph Colegrove, an excitable man who threw himself into every cause he espoused. Frank sent for him and said "I'm in a tight corner. About this bus question—I must hold a meeting tonight—at 7.30—in the Corn Exchange, and it's got to be a success." He produced a slip of paper with the wording on it, and asked how long it would take to get the poster out and how many sandwich men could be marshalled at this short notice. According to Frank's account later, the "light of battle" came into Mr Colegrove's eye and he replied "At 5.30 the posters will be ready and on the boards, and I will have 70 men outside your office and as many as possible will have lamps on them. You will have to break them up for the different districts."

Commenting on this incident, Frank was at his most sententious

124

and used to announce: "There are only two things worth knowing in this world—where to find a thing in a library and the other is to know the right man to do a job."

Another reflection was to the effect that Mr Morris was learning a very elementary lesson "that while it is easy to get a crowd to shout in the street it is difficult to get responsible people to associate with you in an adventure—particularly when you seem certain to lose". However, a city councillor was eventually persuaded to take the chair.

The anxious conspirators had just sat down to dinner in Frank's flat when his chief clerk rushed in and announced that it would be impossible to get near the Corn Exchange because not only was the building packed but every road leading to it was blocked with people trying to get in and the police had failed to move the crowd. "A great load was lifted from my mind", said Frank and the party immediately left the table. Making a detour through the deserted cattle market they went through an emergency door at the back of the Corn Exchange and found themselves on the platform facing a packed audience which broke into a rousing cheer at the sight of them.

It was characteristic of Frank to have put in train a difficult programme without giving a thought to what was to happen if it succeeded, and what he had failed to consider on this occasion was how to satisfy a mob which had come to hear oratory. He said that he was the only man on the platform who could speak for more than five minutes and "I was but an indifferent speaker". (This was ridiculous of the later Frank Gray but it was an honest opinion at the time.) The councillor, in the event, managed to speak for about ten minutes, not inspiringly. Morris would say "I am no speaker" and sit down. A barrister who had been inveigled on to the platform spoke a single sentence and it was left to Frank to put the case for himself and his associates. He afterwards described his speech as "short, bad and unfair". After an unbridled attack on the Corporation, he concentrated his venom on the Town Clerk in an effort to "split their unity". He then went on to attack the National Electric Construction Company in a way which he afterwards thought "unfair and untrue" and he "held up to the crowd" Mr Cownie, the managing director of the company as a man who was intent on robbing Oxford. He said that he and his associates were fighting for them, the people of Oxford, and it was for them, the people of Oxford, to decide whether they wanted this new, modern public service or whether they would allow these two patriotic citizens W. R. Morris and Frank Gray to be hustled off to jail.

Recalling the occasion, Frank described his effort as follows: "It was an inflammatory speech, in a nature inciting to riot." Whether its nature was riot-inciting or not, the crowd was certainly incited for they rushed from the building until they found a tram, turned it over and broke it up; there followed a violent battle with the police as they tried to set fire to the wreckage and although they failed and the police drove them off a far more important victory had been won, Frank thought. "This was the turning point in the fight," he announced with a general's air, "Victory was in sight."

He was over-optimistic but the Corporation was in fact over-awed by the demonstration of public feeling and decided not to take criminal proceedings. They would proceed in Chancery and try to get an injunction to restrain the law breakers, a decision which alarmed Frank because it was obvious that if an injunction was granted nothing could be done until the trial and all public feeling would melt away. Fortunately for the culprits the Corporation procrastinated still further and the application for an injunction was delayed. Mr Cownie now appeared in Oxford and the first thing he did was to threaten Frank with a writ for slander but Frank replied by threatening to bring a libel action because of a reference to him in a letter to the Corporation. At the same time Mr Cownie informed the City Council that if they failed to comply with their contract and got the Morris buses off the road, he would organise a complete service of motor-buses whether the Corporation wanted them or not.

All these threats and counter-threats helped to divide members of the City Council, some of whom were now letting it be known in public that they sympathised with the Morris–Gray faction, but the two men had a new problem—to match Mr Cownie's threat by putting on a complete service of their own. "At this date," Frank said, "it is safe to say that having already bought and paid for two buses, Morris and I, if called upon to produce £500, would have been hard put to it." The one hope was Gilletts Bank, whose partners agreed to receive Messrs Gray and Morris. Not too hopeful, the young men drove to Banbury to meet the bankers and were staggered by the warmth of the reception. On arrival they were ushered into the partners' room and offered a cigar. On leaving they had a cheque for £8,000.

The problem now was to get the buses. From Banbury they went straight to Coventry, arrived at the Daimler factory at nine o'clock and were received by the General Manager, Works Manager and Sales Manager. Here the atmosphere was frosty. Frank immediately let it be known that they were cash customers but it had no effect. The Daimler officials said they had no difficulty in selling buses, in fact had a waiting list and would be unable to deliver one for three months. But one of them made a tactical slip. He let it be known that he knew Mr Cownie very well and had done business with him. Frank pounced on this and made a violent attack, accusing Daimler's of allowing their business sense to be swayed by personal considerations. How would they like it to be known by the shareholders that they turned good money away in order to do somebody else a favour? No doubt he worked himself up into a violent passion and angered his hearers. But he produced an effect and Daimler's decided to appease him. In the yard were two buses ready for delivery and painted on them in large letters was the word "Salford". Daimler's agreed to change the first syllable to Ox and send the vehicles to Oxford next day complete with drivers. Moreover, the sales manager agreed to go to London next day to see whether he could borrow a few buses from companies which had been his customers so that a complete fleet for Oxford could be assembled. Such was the power of Frank's personality when he was confronted by an apparently hopeless situation. He and Morris got back to Oxford at 3.30 in the morning.

The situation began to look hopeful.

Next day, the two buses arrived from Coventry and were

immediately put into service. But, perhaps even more important, the sales manager of Daimler's went into action enthusiastically and more and more buses began to arrive from London with the word "Oxford" hastily painted on them. A second public meeting was held and proved more orderly than the first, but was more impressive since several members of the Council appeared on the platform. At the same time, a monster petition was organised. Tables and chairs were put on the main streets without any objection from the police. In fact, policemen on the beat were actually asked to sign the petition and some did so over and over again. Frank many years later said, "It appeared that the police now regarded the bus question as the Dublin police regarded the political question in 1922—as a matter superior to the law". Fourteen thousand signatures were eventually collected and were taken to the Town Clerk's office in a monster procession. Nobody bothered to check the names. In spite of these encouraging developments Frank was getting restive. There was no sign that the Corporation would give in. They might even make up their minds to enforce the law. And the public was getting bored.

At this point Frank took what he afterwards described as a "bold and dangerous step in which the danger outweighed any possible advantage". There was a well-known Socialist who used to speak in St Giles on Sunday evenings. Frank sent for him and said, "Look here, what are you going to talk about next Sunday? Socialism will fall a bit flat. Everybody is on buses. Why don't you talk about that?" "All right," said the orator. "What do you want me to say?" Frank said, "I don't care what you say but stir them up! Impress the people—regardless of the consequences. You know what to do." The man was to get handbills put around and make sure there was a huge crowd. "You must make it a success and that costs money." Before the interview finished Frank paid the orator £20.

At this time Frank lived in a flat from which he could look down St Giles and on the fateful Sunday he sat in his sitting-room watching the crowd gather. He could hear the distant voice of the speaker and a growing sound of the crowd which laughed repeatedly as the speaker described the feebleness and blundering of the Corporation. The speech developed into a violent attack on the authorities and an incitement to the mob to take action. Men in the audience yelled their head off. When the speech ended the crowd began to sway and turn towards the Cornmarket. It was the way to the Town Hall. Nobody had any clear idea of what was going to happen but the police had formed up to prevent a move to the Town Hall in case anybody had the idea of burning it down. In fact the police behaved with great tact and instead of giving battle they slowly withdrew and led the crowd's leaders down side streets so that eventually what had seemed a united force was broken up into innumerable little groups and the desire for action was lost and dissipated in dozens of harmless arguments. The watching conspirator in his flat commented, "It saved a very ugly situation which it was foolish to have sought to engineer".

Meantime, four of Mr Cownie's buses had arrived. Morris had sixteen, in fact a complete service for the city. Now there was plenty of action to satisfy even Frank. Wherever a Cownie bus appeared the crowd howled and jeered. Anybody who looked like boarding one of these interlopers was jeered at and told to wait for a Morris bus. It required courage to travel on a Cownie vehicle. Passengers were even dragged off and manhandled; conductors and drivers found it impossible to do their jobs. Sometimes Morris buses appeared in pairs, were driven in front of the enemy and brought him to a standstill.

Suddenly it became known that a special meeting of the Council was to be held and this meant that bus licences would at last be granted. But who would get them? Even now the Morris–Gray faction decided on a last attempt at intimidation. All their buses were suddenly taken out of service and driven at top speed to the Town Hall where they drew up so that nobody else could get near. The crowd swarmed on to the Morris buses shouting at the police, at the windows behind which the City Fathers were deliberating and at the interloping buses which now belonged to more than one company for Tillings had arrived in an attempt to share the spoils. But, when at last somebody appeared on the balcony and silence was called for so that the Corporation could announce its decision, it was in fact to declare that the Council had decided to adjourn for two days. There was a loud groan and the mob dispersed to get on with the sport of bus baiting.

Frank and Morris now received an invitation from the Mayor to attend the adjourned meeting and when they did so they were, to their astonishment, shown to places of honour. The Mayor then arose to say that twelve licences would be granted to Mr Morris and twelve to Mr Cownie's company and it was hoped that this would settle the matter once and for all. The verdict was greeted with audible sighs of relief, not least by Frank Gray who had endangered the public peace, inflamed the passions of the mob, and indeed incited to riot, and all not merely to get bus licences for his friend Mr Morris, nor in order to improve the transport system of Oxford but to do something which always counted for more than anything else, as he would have laughingly admitted, and that was simply to get his own way.

But now he did something which was equally characteristic. Without wasting time he left for London and took a cab to Mr Cownie's office. He was met by an office boy who said he would see whether Mr Cownie would see him. But he was so doubtful as to whether he would be received that he hurried after the boy and when a door opened, went in. Cownie looked up, flushed with anger and said, "You have slandered me". Frank said, "Yes, and you have libelled me. Come and have some dinner."

It says much for Mr Cownie's magnanimity that he accepted the invitation. It says much for Frank's power to charm that the meal was a remarkable success. In fact, it went on until midnight and when the two men parted they agreed to dine together again next evening. This was the beginning of a long friendship.

A few days later Messrs Gray and Morris set out for the United States. Morris had been thinking of producing a light motor-car, which eventually turned out to be the Morris Oxford, but had no facilities for producing engines and the cheapest engines available—thanks to Free Trade—were American. Frank said that he was taken along because Morris had developed a great trust in him thanks to the fact that he had brought him "safely through the bus business". The two men were certainly very close at this time, and indeed for some time after the First World War. But here is an example of two friends who quarrelled over politics and became as hostile to each other as they had formerly been intimate. The political issue was Free Trade or Protection. Frank always claimed that Morris' business was built on Free Trade because his car, when it was produced, was made possible by cheap American material; and indeed one of Morris first steps upwards after the bus business was to get the British agency for an American car, the Hupmobile. But, when he had established his business and had the protection of the McKenna Duties, Morris became a convinced Protectionist and the two men were to quarrel violently, and in public, before the astonished audience of the Oxford electorate.

12

Parliamen'

NOT the least surprising development in Oxford life during the First World War was the decision made by Walter Gray, now Sir Walter, to go into Parliament. He had been knighted in 1903, thanks to the fact that he had been mayor in coronation year. He had been mayor on three other occasions. He was recognised as the "father" of Oxford conservatism and Oxford city was now a Conservative seat, its M.P. being Viscount Valentia.[1] Walter's chance came in 1917 when Lord Valentia retired from the House of Commons and Walter assumed that if he applied for the seat he would get it. This, however, was not to be. There was another man who was anxious to get into the House, the historian, J. A. R. Marriott, who took the trouble to get up an impressive speech when he appeared before the Tory selection committee. Walter took no trouble at all. He merely appeared and said he had decided to go into parliamen' (as he still pronounced it). This was not good enough for the committee, which decided to have the University historian. Walter was dumbfounded. To get over his chagrin he decided to take a holiday in Northumberland and died there. On the way back, his manservant mislaid the body, which turned up later on its own. Walter therefore returned for his last visit to Oxford as lonely as he had been on the first.

[1] As an Irish Peer Lord Valentia was allowed to sit in the House of Commons.

There was—and perhaps still is—a tradition among Oxford Conservatives that when Frank went into politics and won the Oxford seat for the Liberal Party he did this because his father had been treated so shabbily by the local Conservatives, that is, out of a desire for revenge. There is no evidence that this was so and Frank strenuously denied it. Of course that is not conclusive. The theory throws doubt on the sincerity of his Liberalism and he could never permit that. But the plain fact is that his war service entirely changed his outlook and made him an enemy of the class privilege for which Conservatism stood.

As a successful lawyer it would have been easy for him to avoid military service entirely, and he had in fact an appointment with the Inland Revenue, thanks to which he was reserved, but he suddenly decided to throw up everything and join up. He joined as a private in the infantry and refused a commission. Never one to do things by halves he refused even a stripe and let it be known that he meant to finish the war as he began it, that is as "Private Gray". When he was in the trenches in France he was offered a transfer to the Transport Command in England but he refused with scorn. He fought and was prepared to die with the men he called "the lowest".

Oddly enough, this gained him little credit with his own class, that is the officer class and, after their quarrel, W. R. Morris attacked him in public for having failed the nation by refusing to take a commission. However, his experience as a private soldier, particularly in the trenches, fixed Frank's destiny and his political outlook. In 1918 he stood as a Liberal candidate at Watford, dealt scornfully with the cry "Hang the Kaiser" and was decisively beaten. But it gave him practice and his eye was on the Oxford constituency, then represented by the ultra-Tory historian J. A. R. Marriott.

After he had given up his legal practice in 1920, Frank had an enormous fund of energy to draw on and he launched a campaign during which he called at every house in Oxford and made friends with everybody who was willing to be a friend. He had an obvious gift for making quick, superficial friendships through banter and a genuine curiosity about other people and he was soon at home even with people who received him with surliness or even hostility.

But his politics was not entirely a personality cult. The war had made him a genuine League of Nations man and and internationalist. He not only did not want to hang the Kaiser but thought it the height of folly to impose harsh peace terms on the Germans.

His anti-Conservatism was increased by a visit to Ireland after the Treaty of 1921. He was on friendly terms with Collins, Griffith, Desmond Fitzgerald and Darrell Figgis. He had been at school with R. C. Barton and through him met Erskine Childers. He got to Dublin in time to see the battle of O'Connell Street where Cartel Bruga died, but what appealed to him was that building operations on the *Freeman's Journal* premises went quietly on while everything near by was being blown up. "My nearest approach to danger," he wrote, "was in the lounge of my hotel when we were suddenly startled by the discharge of a rifle. It was a great relief to discover that it was only one of our Free State Guards who had shot himself by accident."

But it was his experiences in Northern Ireland which influenced him most. He soon reached the conclusion that the members of the Northern Ireland Government were torn between fears for their personal safety and their ambition to start a war involving the British government. He joined a party of journalists, partly local, partly English, and partly American and so managed to see what the Northern Irish Press advertised as "battles". These, he maintained in public speeches, were provoked partly by the Special Constabulary, whose members spent their time trying to get the southerners into a skirmish, and by the size of the British Army on the frontier which was so bored it was spoiling for a fight. The battle of Belleek, hailed throughout Northern Ireland as if comparable with the Marne or the Somme, was fought in such a way that Frank's party managed to cross the British lines without being challenged, much to the fury of the British colonel who arrived later and ordered their arrest. The military tried to make the arrests when the journalistic party was at a small farm sitting down to grilled ham, broad beans and tea. The farmer's family were Northern Irish and pro-British and fervently anti-Southern, but they lied to such good purpose that the military eventually retired having failed to find Frank and his car. What impressed him most about this incident was the evidence that "the Irish are against law and order, whatever the issue".

The British objective was the village of Belleek and, when the signal had been duly received that the southerners had fired first, the British fired a shell towards the village flying the Sinn Fein flag and then advanced to make the momentous capture. According to Frank, "the first sight we saw as we advanced was a party of elderly English fishermen who were very annoyed at us for sending over the shell which fell in the river and disturbed the fish. Otherwise nobody was very much disturbed by this unwonted noise and activity."

He found a more grimly militaristic atmosphere in Belfast where the Prime Minister's residence was defended by trenches and barbed wire entanglement. There was such a state of panic that he saw machine guns turned on firemen, who had to answer 56 calls in a single night. He wrote a letter to the Oxford electors in which he said: "When Northern Ireland was entrusted with a Parliament, they were obsessed with two ideas—one, to create a house as much like the English House of Commons as possible; two, to make it as unlike the English House as possible by eliminating opposition.

"This is how they did it. They got a man, a Sergeant at Arms, and they got a bevy of men dressed in dress suits and gold badges. They proceeded by all the ceremonial and traditional activities associated with the English House of Commons, but they forgot that what is tolerated in a House rich in traditions, interests and surroundings, may be simply laughable when applied to the internal management of six counties.

"Northern Ireland has a large number of Catholics, a minority no doubt but large. The powers that be determined that these people should be neither heard nor seen. The Protestants proceeded to relieve themselves of this opposition by repealing Proportional Representation and then by gerrymandering the constituencies.

"I attended the Northern House of Commons and saw the sad and ridiculous spectacle of sixteen of the dearest old gentlemen sitting amid such pomp and ceremony in Belfast University, all in complete accord with one another so that there was no business left to discuss and nothing to justify them or the 26 overdressed officials."

When he got home he lashed out at more serious targets, in particular Lord Carson. There was no man, he said, for whom he had a more sincere and deep contempt. There was no individual more responsible for the disorder in Ireland during recent times, and for the bloodshed and slaughter of our own soldiers. "He loves to parade himself before his family and immediate circle of friendly admirers as a long-faced stern patriot, prepared to go to the gallows for Ulster, and yet in Ulster's darkest hour when, if at any time, a leader was required, he relinquished that office to a dear old gentleman so that he might take a seat in the House of Lords and a salary of £6,000 a year. Instead of £6,000 a year, it should have been thirty shekels of silver."

There is no record to show what the Oxford electors thought of such rhetoric but it certainly stored up for Frank the wrath of Ulster which was to be hurled at him in a future election.

He was adopted as Liberal candidate for Oxford city when the Lloyd George coalition collapsed in 1922.[1] His candidature was received at first with a certain kindly tolerance among his father's old friends, as can be seen from the pages of the Conservative *Oxford Times*, whose proprietor had been one of Walter's closest and most valuable friends. There was no nonsense about "fairness" in newspaper reporting in those days, and the *Oxford Times*, after a week of campaigning, published three and a half columns of Conservative speeches and half a dozen lines about Frank's adoption. The paper described him as "young, full of good cheer, ready to support all local causes, has taken a great deal of trouble to make friends with his fellow citizens, their wives and families. . .".

But this was not all, for he soon proved himself an effective, in fact magnetic speaker who drew the crowds and entertained

[1] Frank Gray stood as a staunch Asquithian.

them. He had an original bantering style and his hearers always knew they would have some fun. He began one of his earliest speeches by announcing that, before coming to points of constructive policy, he proposed to "poke a little fun" at his opponents. A Conservative speaker had eulogised Mr Marriott (the Conservative member) for his success in the House of Commons and what Frank meant by poking fun was to express surprise that a government which obviously had great difficulty in finding suitable occupants for its offices failed to call on this genius, the member for Oxford city.

This was followed by an analysis of Mr Marriott's voting record, which was not at all good, and then Frank worked himself up into a state of indignation and said that the tributes to Mr Marriott were "audacity which amounted to cheek".

It was because of this kind of speech that the Conservatives accused him of introducing "personalities", and one of his opponents denounced him for running "cheapjack" meetings. However, he not only lashed out in a way which the crowd loved but was always able to appear as the victim of dirty tactics by the other side. On one occasion he alleged that his enemies were spreading the report that he had turned out two old ladies from a cottage in St Ebbe's. "I am one of the largest property owners in Oxford," he declared indignantly. "I have never in my life served a notice to quit on anybody." (A voice, "Only Marriott".) They had also spread the rumour that he was a "pussyfoot" which was absurd. (Loud laughter.) But he was vastly encouraged. It was like boxing: "The moment you see one fighter trying to hit below the belt you know he has lost."

His chief object in standing for Parliament, he announced, was to cleanse public life. He would like to have a list of those gentlemen who, although in receipt of pensions worth over £350 a year had been given jobs in the Government: then everybody would know who were the friends and relations of the coalitionists. There was no Labour candidate in this election but Frank was the friend of Labour. There was a great effort on the Conservative side to show that the Labour Party was positively un-British because it drew funds from foreign sources. Let the other parties be made to say where their money came from! Let every candidate be compelled to reveal the source of his election expenses! If he were returned to the House of Commons his first act would be to draft a one-clause bill making it compulsory for all subscribers to political associations to register at Somerset House under the Companies Act.

Whether it was this line of attack or simply the preliminary work he had done before the campaign, it began to be evident that he was not a freak candidate but somebody who might win. He addressed 13 separate meetings on the eve of the poll. Next day he was out at dawn and started to call at every house in the constituency. In the afternoon he drove to the station to wait for railway workers who had been working down the lines and presently a train drew up decorated in the Liberal colours of red and white, and with the slogan "Gray for Oxford" painted along the length of a carriage. The workers formed a procession and headed by their hero made for the nearest polling station. As they passed under the first bridge plate-layers swarmed on the parapet and shouted "Rely on us".

It was a foggy November day but people sat outside their houses waiting to see Frank Gray. As night fell he went through the worst slums; people brought out candles and ran to get a glimpse of him. The most remarkable scenes occurred behind the brewery where Squire Hall once decided to fight Harcourt. Here there were hordes of children with mouth-organs, tin-whistles, trombones and an old drum. The band formed up, Frank came next and then a mob of people, who all marched to the Town Hall. He was in his element.

The first candidate to be declared elected was the under-graduate candidate Julia Jorrocks, this declaration being made from a pub opposite the Town Hall. But even more remarkable was the genuine result announced from the Town Hall itself. Frank had polled over 12,000 votes against Marriott's 8,683, and so the Conservative majority of 5,000 won in 1918 was turned into a minority of 3,806. It was said that the beaten Tory historian was so upset that he failed to shake hands with the victor. The crowd went mad. Frank was carried to the Reform Club where he announced that the result would resound throughout the whole of England. "It will stand as the beacon of progress. It is the biggest victory that has ever been won in Oxford."

The Conservatives were puzzled. The *Oxford Times* sadly reproached the electors for having forgotten that there was a difference between real politicians like Mr Marriott, who were born to legislate, and this agreeable young man who would be out of place at Westminster and "much more useful at home". However, the situation was still comparatively friendly and Frank now hurled himself into the task of proving that he was not merely a useful local young man but a born legislator.

As soon as he got into Parliament he started an agitation to give the vote to the wives of heads of colleges, and was successful. There was something peculiarly Frankish in this move because he knew perfectly well that, so far as Oxford was concerned, most of the newly enfranchised ladies would certainly vote against him, but this consideration added to the merit of his action. In other ways he declared war on the University for he was outraged by its archaic privileges.

The most remarkable of these privileges was an exclusive jurisdiction in civil matters, superior to the High Courts. According to a Charter of Henry IV, confirmed by Elizabeth I and tested in the case Rex v. Agar, 1772, it could claim criminal jurisdiction including the right to try capital offences, and Frank maintained that, according to this charter, if a member of the University ran over somebody anywhere in the United Kingdom the victim would be deprived of all remedy and relief in the High Court of Justice. There had, in fact, been a test case within his own lifetime, in 1885, when a circus owner called Ginnett brought an action for libel against an undergraduate called Whittingham who had published certain statements in the *Daily Chronicle*, *Pall Mall Gazette* and *Pall Mall Budget*. Mr Ginnett served a writ but the undergraduate's guardian, who knew the law pretty well, took it to the University solicitor who went to the Vice-Chancellor and as a result the matter was judged by Lord Chief Justice Coleridge who announced that "we" were not insensible of the "grave inconveniences which might follow from allowing this claim of connusance", in fact that "we" might regret the action of the University authorities in insisting on a claim which belonged to a state of things which had passed away but that "we" did not make the statute of Elizabeth and there it was. In other words, nobody could sue a member of the University in the ordinary courts.

This was the most extreme example of University power but it was not the only one, for the Vice-Chancellor could ban any local place of entertainment and order a raid on the railway to Oxford, powers which were still exercised in Frank's day when Oxford was more or less dominated by the "banning Vice-Chancellor", Dr Farnell, who at one time tried to close down the Oxford Playhouse. Frank tirelessly opposed these absurd anachronisms and became known as an enemy of the University for his pains.

He was the prototype of a new member of Parliament. He never missed a division. Every Friday evening, he leaped into a taxi from Westminster to Paddington, travelled to Oxford and rushed to his office where there was always a queue of constituents waiting to tell him their troubles. But this was not enough. He rushed off to the Ruhr, to Russia and to Poland and poured his impressions into the *Oxford Chronicle*. But what brought him most publicity was a stunt which probably affected his health for the rest of his life. As Private Gray he had suffered the fantastic weight of the equipment an ordinary soldier in the infantry was forced to carry and, having failed to make any impression on the War Office, he publicly challenged any man of his age—forty-two—or older to race him from Banbury to Oxford, 23 miles, in full marching order, infantry equipment. The challenge was accepted by the member for Bury, Captain Ainsworth, who was forty-nine and the national Press whipped up the country into a fever of excitement.

At seven o'clock on the morning of 27th August 1923, the two men slung regulation rifles on their backs, plus packs weighing 70 lbs each, and set off from Banbury to the Martyrs' Memorial in Oxford. The road was wet but the rain had stopped and the marchers made good progress. They were attended by a few other walkers and a lot of cyclists. At Deddington, villagers broke into cheers, for Frank was well known and motorists began to fall in behind. Half-way to Oxford, Captain Ainsworth took the lead but suddenly decided to take a rest and threw off his equipment. Frank followed suit but got going again first. Nevertheless the betting was on Captain Ainsworth for the next few miles because his lengthy stride was thought better than Frank's infantry marching, and the older man did take the lead until he had to stop to take his boots off. Seven miles from Oxford near his own home Frank was in distress but struggled on to the city boundary where he threw off his pack and flung himself on the ground. A few minutes later, when his opponent passed him, he got to his feet and set off at a ridiculous pace only to collapse at the railway crossing. The two men were now both in such distress that the crowd became alarmed about the outcome. Captain Ainsworth collapsed finally at the end of the Banbury Road, but Frank, by a series of desperate efforts, managed to get to the Martyrs' Memorial where he in turn collapsed. He was carried into the Randolph Hotel where the porter, asked for his opinion by the Press said, "Well, all I can say is— it's a rum show." It was the kind of rum show which did Frank harm for it earned him the reputation of being a mere showman.

13

Overdoing it

FRANK had certainly shown his prowess as an electioneer, but he was to show it even more effectively in the next election, in November 1923,[1] which was to prove not only the most spectacular contest in the country but one of the most spectacular in the history of the Oxford constituency. It may have lacked the public disorder of the nineteenth-century elections but even they lacked the degree of personal bitterness which dwarfed every other element. This was because the two old friends, Frank and W. R. Morris, suddenly became bitter and remorseless enemies. The difference was ostensibly over Protection, under which Morris had built up his business; where he had been turning out 500 cars a year in 1914 he was now turning out 500 a week and where he had employed 150 men he now employed 3,000. But the question of tariffs merely provided the argument. What provided the temper was the personal clash.

The most extraordinary allegation made against Frank was that, although he had fought in the trenches during the war, he had proved himself a traitor to his country because he had failed to accept a commission! The allegation was extraordinary, not only because his conduct in this respect seemed to many people particularly brave and unselfish but because it proved the prime tactical blunder made by Mr Morris who first brought the matter

[1] Baldwin had become Prime Minister in May, announced his belief in Protection and went to the country for a mandate.

into the open. Frank was given a glorious opportunity to demonstrate how he had stayed with the people when they were deserted by everybody who could wangle a commission or a soft job at home; he was also able to retort that he had never attacked Mr Morris for not joining up at all, thus mentioning the matter without appearing an utter cad. But the exchange of abuse on this subject had a deep significance. Frank's real offence in the eyes of his opponents was not that he was a Free Trader but that he had deserted his own class. He was a rich man, a public school man, a highly successful business man and lawyer who ought to have been in the forefront in the fight for privilege. The odd thing was that the man who voiced the resentment against him was an entirely self-made man. In some mysterious way the two classes seemed to have reversed themselves.

The campaign started with a rumour that W. R. Morris himself would stand as the Conservative candidate and, in fact, Frank wrote to him urging him to do so and ending with the words, "Of course I would have preferred a walk-over to fighting you, but I am sure a fight will not disturb our many years of intimate friendship". In the end Morris declined because of ill-health and the honour went to a young man, R. C. Bourne, a rowing blue who eventually became Deputy Speaker of the House of Commons. This brought a derisive blast from Frank, who referred to his opponent as a young man who had been brought down to drag the chestnuts out of the fire for the men who spent their time at the County Club "sipping their port wine and concocting their little plots against him, who by education and fortune and by any other test were as eligible as he to serve the great country to which they owed allegiance". What did it mean to be an M.P.? Since he was elected himself he had known no home life. He had attended every sitting of the House and on Fridays he took a taxi and dashed to the station so that he could be at the Oxford Town Hall at six o'clock to answer questions. He received 70 letters a day. Every one was answered and nobody had been refused an interview. There was scarcely an organisation in Oxford of which he was not President, and he was proud of the duties and honour, but he could not disguise from himself that Oxford was becoming a one-man show and there were definite limits as to what one man could do. . . . It was indictment against County and City that men who had made fortunes or inherited them did not come in and share with him the responsibility and anxiety and work of public life. If the Conservative candidate had arrived merely in the hope of getting a little social advancement or merely to keep him, Frank Gray, from going to another constituency and helping somebody else, he ventured to suggest that the electors might have been spared the expense.

It was good rousing stuff, interrupted by cheer after cheer, and containing just that touch of arrogance or insolence which his supporters adored and which made his enemies tremble with fury. The allegation that the important men of the Conservative party were a lot of cowardly port-sippers who let the country down by failing to provide him, Frank Gray, with a worthy opponent was just what was needed to get the campaign off to a flying start.

On the central issue of the national election, Tariff Reform, Frank at first took up the position that Morris Motors Ltd., because of the duty on foreign cars, was in a privileged position which would disappear if there was general protection, but in reply to a letter sent by Morris he said that, if the threat of general protection was beaten off, he thought he "could afford to co-operate with Mr Morris to get this local benefit, at the expense of others". Morris was not satisfied with this and began to take an active part in the campaign and ask questions. Frank wrote and suggested a meeting on a public platform but had no reply. At one of Frank's first meetings in the campaign, he was interrupted and said, "I have invited you to meet me on a platform, Mr Morris, and have had no reply". (Voices: "Good old Frankie" and "Chuck him out".) "Mr Morris is not to be chucked out", said Frank, pointing to the arches under the hall, "When you embark on general tariff reform, there will be a Mr Morris in every one of those arches, all of them asking, 'Where do I come in' and I don't blame them". There was more interruption from the men with Morris and Frank said, "All in good time. I don't understand your anger, Mr Morris." When Frank again referred to his offer to take part in a debate with Morris and said he was sure Mr Morris would oblige him, the other men shouted, "Most decidedly".

At a later meeting Frank launched his attack on Morris on the ground that he was using politics to put his business before the national interest. At a Conservative meeting, Morris said that if protection for the motor-car industry came to an end a thousand men at Cowley would have to be sacked. "That is the policy of the squire of two hundred years ago," Frank declaimed. "It would be impossible for me to meet these men in his works without endangering their employment." No doubt the motor manufacturer was sincere in thinking his business would be ruined if it was exposed to the full blast of competition, but being no politician he had exposed himself to the blast of a real politician, who was able to quote his words again and again in order to show that the Morris workers would be victimised and those who voted Liberal would be sacked. Frank threw all his indignation into this, "'My business'. There are men and women who are about to be evicted from their cottages, there are police pensioners with grievances, old-age pensioners with grievances, temperance reformers who claim attention, licensed victuallers whose case they desire me to consider. There are the great national interests. Kingdoms may rise and fall. 'My business'. Never, I venture to say to you, was a political platform put to such disgraceful purposes in the history of this country."

It is easy to laugh at such rhetoric, and Frank would have laughed if it had been quoted to him afterwards, but in point of fact he was proclaiming a revolutionary doctrine and one which his opponents—especially W. R. Morris—refused to believe, to wit, that the interest of a big business man and the public were not necessarily synonymous. He said this in so many words and Morris, dumbfounded, could only say, "Well, that's news to me".

Frank alleged that Morris had imported a "gang of paid men" from Coventry to interrupt his meetings. It was at one meeting where he first made this allegation that he quietened the hubbub by saying, "I am watching your faces and one man I am going

K   145

to pick out—I have picked him out already", with the result that the wretched man was intimidated into leaving. When he repeated that the interrupters came from Coventry there were shouts of "Liar" but Frank said, "I know everybody in Oxford by sight" and it was recognised as true. When the meeting had finished he turned on them his best grin and said, "I thought you would come to love me".

Frank at various times declared that the Oxford election had become a "huge joke" and an "astounding situation". The Tory candidate was completely forgotten and "the only man who counted was Mr Morris who said he was ill, who got a man to do battle for him, and then ruthlessly shoved him aside so that the limelight should be shed on Mr Morris". He, Frank Gray, was pitted against "Mr Morris and his hooligans, who were going to crack his head because they could not answer his arguments".

He was taunted by Mr Morris "as being a traitor to my country because I refused a commission in the Army when there was a call for officers and preferred to remain a private". That, he confessed, was perfectly true. While he was in the trenches he was offered the rank of captain and the control of motor transport in England. He refused it. He held it was not right to desert the men who actually saved his life in France. "I have never attacked Mr Morris for not going, I attack no man for not going into the Army, but I shall defend myself."

Frank now mounted an attack on Morris on the ground that he had been a Free Trader when it suited him and had abandoned what he believed in because of "his business". This was based on the fact that Morris first went to America before the war in order to buy American motor-car engines to put in the Morris Oxford. Frank went on that visit to America with him: "He had a great belief in me then because I had got him safely through the bus controversy." Morris was the first agent in Britain for the American Hupmobile and had "by importing and selling American cars alone made a fortune". On the occasion of the last election it was Mr Morris who supplied him with a car, and it was American.

When Mr Morris tried to defend himself at a Conservative meeting he had difficulty in getting a hearing and cries of "Frank Gray! Frank Gray!" provided a running accompaniment. He was indignant at the charge that he might victimise his men. He had tried all his life to create employment, "and I ask you what has Mr Gray created?" If the Liberals supported Protection he would support them. Without Protection it was impossible to absorb unemployment. He was giving the motor production figures when his voice was drowned by the uproar in the hall: interrupters were thrown out at intervals to cries of "another one gone". At the end Mr Morris was chaired from the Corn Exchange to his garage.

A new source of excitement was introduced by the arrival of four M.P.s from Northern Ireland to support the Conservatives and abuse Frank in such terms that the local Press was afraid to report most of their oratory. They were led by a certain Alderman Duff who made the sinister allegation that Frank went into the kitchens and "shared bloaters with working men's wives". Alderman Duff continually referred to the Liberal candidate as "Private Gray". "Private Gray tried to 'culuminate' and throw mud at anybody who happened to disagree with him. At the first meeting I listened to," said Alderman Duff, "he tried to create a class war between private and officer, the most dishonourable and disreputable thing I have ever listened to, even in Ireland. Frank Gray had put out a poster—'a miserable cowardly poster'—shouting, 'I am being persecuted. I have not only to fight Captain Bourne, but I have to fight Mr Morris, and I have to fight Mr Morris's workmen, who are paid for their dirty work' ". Having quoted this, Alderman Duff referred to Private Gray as "a miserable hound". He was sure that Frank Gray would get the surprise of his life because "working men are not bought with cigarettes" and members of the British Legion would not "sell their votes for occasional drinks"—these, presumably, being Frank's methods of bribery. Alderman Duff ended with the declaration: "There is not an artifice of electioneering and there is not a dirty trick of electioneering that Frank Gray has not tried during this election." After which, the *Oxford*

Chronicle reported Alderman Duff with the following comment: "We give these vulgar and stupid sentences in order that the public may realise the sort of opposition which Mr Gray has had to fight. The matter is obviously libellous and we have only published it after getting a formal indemnity from Mr Gray." (How glad Mr Gray was to give it may be judged from the fact that he was virtually the owner of the newspaper.)

The origin of his squabble with Ulster lay in a visit which he paid to that country in 1922. He had passports for both North and South Ireland, crossed the frontier several times and, when he came back to England, he testified that the Northern Ireland Special Constabulary, which cost the English taxpayer a million and a half pounds a year, was fond of sniping on the frontier in the hope of provoking Southern reprisals and that he himself had seen two pitched battles. At the same time the British Army there was too big and by persistently raising the subject in Parliament he had had it reduced from ten battalions to four. But the waste of money on the Special Constables went on and he pulled no punches in describing them. He blamed them for the reign of terror which he saw in Belfast, "a reign of arson and bloodshed". He saw firemen when they were trying to do their job "having machine guns turned on them". He slept one night in the Belfast fire station; there were 56 calls and 12 factories were burned down. He described the Special Constables as "an immoral and disgraceful lot responsible in a large number of cases for the murder of Catholics". That is why they hated him and sent four M.P.s across in an effort to unseat him. He was vilified week after week in the Irish papers. He was always receiving abusive letters and active threats, but he announced at one meeting that he would give his reply after the election by going to Ulster and speaking there. However, the abuse from Alderman Duff and the others was useful to him because all he had to do was read out reports of their language in order to startle even his Conservative hearers, and of course he made great play with the fact that Captain Bourne was allowing such tactics. In one speech, he referred to the interlopers as "four members of Parliament, at whose expense I know not, but apparently when you have decided you cannot win an election, any illegality, any unauthorised proceeding is permissible" and again, "it passes my comprehension that anybody . . . should do so dangerous a thing as to bring men here to vilify me as though I were already a convicted criminal".

On the eve of the poll he held a series of meetings, which were described as the greatest political demonstration ever known in Oxford. The Town Hall was packed, part of the overflow moved into the Assembly Room, and it was then decided to throw open the Drill Hall beneath the Town Hall. Even so, a crowd of over a thousand people stood in the street hoping to see him and shouting for him. He spoke in all three halls and finally left his supporters because some time before he had agreed to make a final speech for the Liberal candidate in south Oxfordshire.

When the police were forcing a way for him from one meeting to another, a woman rushed forward to embrace him and said, "Don't overdo it, Frank, you're winning all right".

He won (by 12,311 votes to 9,618) but he had certainly overdone it.

14

"Worse still—found out"

IT is possible he thought nothing was wrong; in fact it is certain for two judges afterwards found him not guilty of corrupt practice. His explanation of what happened during the 1923 election campaign and, particularly what led ultimately to his being unseated, would have been credible, one might have thought, only to somebody who had known him well and for a long time. Everything Frank did was a one-man performance and so it was with his method of conducting an election. Everything centred on him or was inspired by him. He was inexhaustibly energetic and thought he could do everything himself. The corollary to this was that other people lost sight of what they ought to be doing, in this case the drudgery work of book-keeping, getting estimates for printing and propaganda and above all keeping within the election law. This is what had been disastrously neglected.

The few weeks after the election were triumphant because he was acclaimed as the most spectacular winner in the whole election and he was made a Junior Whip. The radical periodical, *The Nation*, referred to him as one of the most popular men in the House and he was in good form in reporting to his constituents on the importance of Parliamentary work, "We haven't had time to solve unemployment. Housing is a complicated problem and we haven't had quite enough time for that. But we have voted ourselves £70,000 for our railway fares." In point of fact, this was a moment of peculiar excitement in Parliamentary affairs because Mr Baldwin's Conservative Party had polled less than the combined Liberals and Labour Party and the country was on the brink of its first Labour government.

But it suddenly dawned on Frank that he had something more pressing to worry about than the Parliamentary tactics of his party. One day in the House of Commons he overheard a member say it was the last day for making a return of election expenses. This was wrong, there was still a week left, but Frank did not know that and rushed back to Oxford to see whether his agent had made the return. The fact that he had not bothered about this before is extraordinary in itself and there was a good deal of incredulity afterwards that a man who had been a practising solicitor could have been so careless and improvident. But it was typical of him. He left drudgery to others.

The man who was supposed to look after this side of the campaign was a young man called Johnstone, who had been Frank's captain during the war. He had no experience as a political agent and knew nothing about election law, though he bought a book and started to read it up. He came to live at Shipton Manor as a secretary and when the election writ was served Frank asked him to be his agent. But although Mr Johnstone was officially known as the Liberal agent and carried out his duties satisfactorily so far as the arrangement of meetings was concerned, he never seems to have had the authority to supervise the whole operation, even if he had had the experience to do so. For instance, the cheques were signed by Mrs Gray, who hated to have a bill lying about and sent off a cheque as soon as possible, sometimes for bills which ought to have been included in the election account. Further, Frank relied for many things on the charming, studious and devoted editor of the *Oxford Chronicle*, Percy Linaker, who was also joint secretary of the Liberal Association, and used the newspaper valiantly to further the Liberal cause, by publishing for instance a special edition on the eve of the election, almost entirely devoted to Frank's candidature and all done without charge.

That his various organisers and helpers had not produced an

absolutely perfect result was evident to Frank when he asked about the election return and was told that they had overspent by £2, os. 1d. This made him very angry but he seems to have thought no more about it for his agent went on living at Shipton and the two men were busy preparing a newspaper which was to be called *Ariel*. Nevertheless, the rumours of a petition continued and finally, in February, it was filed by J. H. Morrell, a member of the brewing family, and Alderman Hugh Hall, brother of Squire Hall who was unseated in 1881: Alderman Hall was a leader-writer on the Conservative *Oxford Times* and may have felt a little apprehensive when Frank won control of that paper, but it was one of the occasions when he could justifiably claim that he "bore malice to no man".

It was not until after the filing of the petition that Frank had a grand inquiry into the conduct of the election and realised the magnitude of the disaster. The petitioners claimed that certain items which ought to have been included in the election expenses had not even been mentioned. First of all, before the date of the election was known, Frank had some cards printed to celebrate the anniversary of his original election. These bore his photograph and the inscription, "A year ago you did not forget me and I will not forget you". Eight thousand of these cards were distributed after the writ for the new election was issued and the petitioners claimed therefore that they were an expense. That was something that could be argued about and might be disposed of.

A little more difficult was the free distribution of the *Oxford Chronicle*. It was almost entirely a propaganda sheet and, although the normal paper was published on a Friday, this had come out on the Wednesday, obviously in order to influence votes. Frank himself suggested this issue and Mr Linaker had thrown himself into the job with a right good will. Nine thousand copies were given away.

But far more serious than these enterprises was the actual cooking of the accounts. To his horror Frank learned that without the postcards and the *Oxford Chronicle*, he had overspent by far more than £2, os. 1d. and that his agent and collaborators had made a series of determined assaults on the proper figures in order to get them down to two pounds plus the disarming penny. What Mr Johnstone did when he discovered the magnitude of the overspending was to go to one of the printers, Joseph Colegrove, the Mr Colegrove who had come to Frank's aid in the bus dispute of 1912, and ask him if he would reduce his charge by accepting some "returns", chiefly boxes of envelopes sent to Shipton Manor before the election. No appeal for help ever went unheeded by Mr Colegrove if he thought Frank would benefit and he readily agreed to the amount suggested by the agent. What is more, in making out a cheque for the return of the money, he put a date on the cheque suggested by Mr Johnstone, who wanted to make it seem that the reduced amount was agreed originally and so was the correct figure for the election return.

Mr Johnstone then went to Mr Linaker of the *Oxford Chronicle* confided in him and asked for his help. The *Oxford Chronicle* had done a certain amount of the printing, had submitted a bill for £180 and received a cheque for that amount. Mr Johnstone and Mr Linaker, however, now studied the account, reduced some of the items, and even abolished some of the others—such as the charge for advertisements—with the result that the bill was reduced to £118 and a receipt for this amount was dated back to 27th December, because that was the date of the cheque already paid. What was more, the books of the *Oxford Chronicle* were altered, although they had already been examined by the auditors.

There were several other allegations which would not be easily disposed of, such as the hiring of cars without including the charges, the insuring of cars lent for polling day and the question whether proper charges had been made for ward helpers and men who distributed the newspapers and postcards. But the jiggery pokery in the *Oxford Chronicle* books was the most serious.

Frank was aghast. He said he strode up and down his room wringing his hands and said, "My God! I will write to the people on the other side and tell them everything and I will apply for the Chiltern Hundreds." But that would be no solution. He had signed the affidavit swearing his election return was true, but he had taken no steps to find out whether it was, and if he had taken the simplest step such as looking at the *Oxford Chronicle* books he would have known that elaborate steps had been taken to falsify it. As for his relations with Mr Johnstone, Frank said, "I sulked every time he came into the room and said, 'I don't know whether I get on your nerves or you on mine. You had better go away for the weekend.'" However, Mr Johnstone returned after the week-end and was still living at Shipton when the petition was heard in May.

In his own account of the hearing, Frank said, "Everybody on my side desired to say at the outset, 'We know we've done wrong, and worse still we've been found out. Take the seat away please and don't say anything more about it.'" But petitions are not conducted in that way. There were two judges, Messrs Sankey and Swift, and an army of K.C.s, headed by Mr Cecil Whitely for the petitioners and Mr J. B. Matthews for the defence. The days before the hearing put a new strain on Frank's nerves because he discovered that everybody involved in such a case treats his or her evidence as by far the most important. The most childish incident in this case was the purchase of three flannel bulldogs which adorned Frank's car, were stolen by some undergraduates and replaced by some more. They bore the inscription, "I need no Protection", and were made by a parson's wife who, when she discovered that the bulldogs ought to have been charged as an election expense, took to waylaying Frank wherever possible, sometimes when he was going into a hall to make a speech, in an effort to consult him about some new evidence which she thought she could give on the burning question of the flannel bulldogs.

According to Frank a number of people left Oxford until the petition was over and he claimed there was one man who wished he had followed their example. This is the story as told by him, though it does not appear in the official transcript.

"He was sitting in court among my enemies—who attended regularly like spectators at the gladiators' show, with thumbs down—when one of the judges sternly said to a witness, 'Who gave you that letter?' It did not matter who had given him the letter, nor in fact whether the letter had ever been given at all, but the witness was not to know that and, looking wildly round the court, his eyes suddenly sparkled and with extended hand he pointed to a man who had nothing to do with the case and said, 'That's the gentleman'. It is no exaggeration to say that this allegation caused a sensation in Court. The gentleman in question, observed by all, turned a deathly white, which appeared to confirm the frightful charge that it was he who had given the letter. Up to this time he had been a regular and interested spectator, but he did not return to the Court after the adjournment for lunch and was never seen in the vicinity again."

Frank claimed that one of the witnesses said to him, "We shall all have to tell the truth—but not in too naked a form", and he made a note about his counsel who, he said, "embarked upon many and varied explanations, all of which tended to add confusion and doubt, for he knew that while the court could be kept on these innocent matters, a lot more serious matters might escape discussion. So they did!" What they were he never explained.

The heart of the matter was the reduction of the *Oxford Chronicle* account, or in other words the cooking of its books. Mr Linaker, the editor, was asked whether Mr Johnstone, when he asked for a reduction, mentioned the reason and he replied, "It may be said to have been tacitly avoided", a very characteristic observation. There was considerable confusion as to how the alterations were made. First, Mr Linaker thought he had given the cashier a list of the 13 alterations to be made, then he returned to the box to say that the changes were marked in pencil on the ledger which the cashier took home so that he could make them in red ink, but afterwards this was altered to black ink after which a not very successful attempt was made to rub out the pencil marks. The cashier was a Mr Gould who was referred to by Mr Justice Swift as follows: "He is the gentleman who keeps running for books and things. At present he is out of court. He has gone after another ledger." It was Gould who admitted he had altered the books after they had been audited and was told by the Judge "If you will take my advice, you will never do so again".

Frank said, "Mr Gould was made the scapegoat, and it must be confessed that his evidence, and his manner of giving it, supplied all the necessary suspicion. He was repeatedly threatened with imprisonment, although he was probably the most upright and innocent man present—not excluding the judges. First, from beginning to end, he did not know what they were talking about. And then he was anxious to take all the blame, whether it was due to him or not."

Mr Gould was exonerated in one particular. Everybody thought he had been careless in failing to rub out the pencil marks efficiently, when suddenly Mr J. B. Matthews, K.C., revealed that he was the guilty person. On looking through the accounts he had realised they were not even added up correctly and made a pencil note in the margin; then he realised he was tampering with an original document and tried to rub it out. He offered to take off his wig and gown and go into the witness box but the judges refused permission, according to Frank, because they had already heard ten different explanations from Mr Matthews. He had a reputation for long-windedness and according to one story had been addressed by a judge in the following terms: "Do you think you could tell us whether you appear for the Plaintiff or the Defendant, without undue verbosity." In this case he was asked by the judges if he could answer in "a few words" while after one of his speeches, Mr Justice Swift said, "I thank you for giving me the reasons for the decision I have already announced". (Laughter.)

Frank had decided to bare his breast in public and gave a dramatic demonstration of bearing malice to no man. He referred to Mr Linaker as his "guide, philosopher and friend", and this relationship lasted until death. So far from blaming Mr Johnstone, he blamed himself for having led him into a situation which might ruin him. "I think I was very wrong to appoint him . . . I bitterly regret the whole thing. I had neglected the whole thing from beginning to end." This magnanimity was not shared by Mr Johnstone. He admitted he had categorically told Frank that the accounts were correct but when he was asked, "Are you grateful to Mr Gray", he replied "For what?" However, this exchange was interpreted by the prosecution as the result of a pact: Mr Johnstone took the blame and Frank in return put up a public profession of responsibility. Mr Whitely finally said that if in fact Frank did not know the accounts were cooked he "wilfully abstained from knowing".

However, this was too subtle for the judges. Mr Johnstone was found guilty of corrupt practices, but Frank was not guilty. He had been an "honest and truthful witness" and while he must lose the seat his honour was untarnished.

He was received with cheers when he left the Court and was followed by a crowd to the Clarendon Hotel.

15

Substitutes

IN 1929, just before Frank's fiftieth birthday, the following appeared in the *Oxford Mail*:

"Frank Gray was once described in Parliament as the Peter Pan of politics. He fought four elections, sat in two Parliaments and was unseated on petition, all within five years. He was back-bencher and front-bencher in less than a year. Not bad going!

"With such a record he would find it difficult to deny that he had ever been a politician, though he may wish to, I should think he has spent considerable time in covering up his tracks.

"But at least he has been something more than a politician. He has been a lawyer, with honours, the holder of legal appointments, a commercial man, director of steam laundries, gas companies, hotel and restaurant companies, picture palaces, engineering, building and contracting companies, a soldier—only a private—organiser of international and other information research work, a traveller and explorer, a leader of agricultural labourers, the winner of wagers, athlete, journalist at home and abroad, author, farmer and landowner, an agricultural labourer, Warwickshire miner and a tramp. For all I know, my list may not be complete.

"He cannot truthfully be said to have been a complete failure at any of these occupations. Indeed, on occasions he has shown ability, and on many fewer occasions he has shown flashes of brilliancy. What is more, he is the unconscious possessor of one positive virtue—he bears malice to no man.

"Some of his friends ask, and all his enemies ought to ask, what would have happened had he given his sole undivided unswerving and continued attention to any of these activities. It is difficult to think what he would have become if he had merely been as generous to himself as he is to others.

"One of these days—when he has grown up—he may concentrate on one object. Then he will become a danger to his enemies and cease to be a danger to himself."

Most of this disingenuous stuff was written by Frank, who was contributing a series of character sketches under a pseudonym, but I wrote the conclusion ignoring the fact that he prided himself on not having any enemies.

It was true, as he said in his autobiography, that after he was kicked out of politics he tried a dozen ways of using his energy, but while each experiment absorbed him for a time it never led anywhere.

He needed physical outlets and tried a little exploring, for instance in the Andes and in the Sahara, where he drove a Jowett car in a gruelling journey. But more difficult as a physical test was his effort to become a miner in Warwickshire before the General Strike of 1926. It was a time of serious unemployment when the miners' leader, A. J. Cook, was the bogeyman of the capitalists. Only Frank would have thought it possible to get a job at a pit and, in view of his lack of skill, it was just as well that he failed. But he went to extraordinary lengths in preparing for this new stage in his career which would have qualified him, presumably, to appear in print and on the platform as an expert on the problem of the mines.

He knew a young miner at Nuneaton called Jack and arranged for Jack to move to a new pit, get a job there, work for a fortnight reporting conditions and book lodgings for Frank in a near-by village. This was because Frank was unknown in this particular village and hoped to escape detection. Frank had carefully studied the "leaving costume" as worn by the miner when he went from one job to another, and on the appointed Sunday arrived at the village in his cheap suit and bright pullover, carrying in a bag two filthy shirts and a pair of heavy boots.

He was to stay in the cottage of a Mr and Mrs Parsons. This consisted of a room and scullery on the ground floor and three small bedrooms upstairs. The Parsons had five children from twelve to one and six dogs. Just before nightfall, to Frank's astonishment a girl of sixteen arrived to sleep in the house because it was less crowded than that occupied by her parents on the other side of the road. This meant ten people to sleep.

After tea, bread and jam, the grown-ups all went to the local pub to spend the evening. As Frank said, "Where else could they spend it?" The most important man in the pub was the bookie and the sole topic of conversation was horse-racing. Up to this moment Frank thought he had had all the experience necessary to a man of the world, but he marvelled at the gambling mania in this mining village and particularly at the worship of the bookie. Mr Parsons as a miner earned 50s. a week and of this he set aside 5s. for gambling, 10 per cent. This was not a secret vice. The men were encouraged by their wives, and Frank heard one woman soundly berating her husband because he had forgotten to put a bet on a horse which lost. The woman was not concerned about the money saved. Her husband's remissness had broken some sort of magic.

Every morning at dawn Frank trudged to the pit-head and queued with genuine miners only to be snarled at by the foreman: "Don't want them we've got." Mrs Parsons, when he reported failure to her for the fifth day, said, "If I had my way I would make the bloody swells dig every bit of coal they wanted for a dinner before they had one". On another occasion she cried and said she would take him to Coventry to meet her brother who worked in the Triumph cycle works and could surely get him a job.

The sympathy was touching but living conditions were grim. Since he and Jack paid a pound a week each as lodgers, Mrs Parsons felt rich but all the available money was spent at once. For the first few days of the week badly cooked joint followed badly cooked joint and then it was bread and margarine. In a near-by cottage there were four working sons and a husband bringing in more than ten pounds a week which the housewife spent on the dearest joints. These, whatever their size, were all chopped into equal portions which were plonked on the half-dozen plates to be either eaten or thrown away. After a few weeks Frank abandoned his ambition to be a miner and went back to Shipton Manor. In his effort to renew that communion with "the lowest", which he had experienced during the war, he had failed.

Soon afterwards he tried again, this time as a tramp. He spent an enormous amount of time rehearsing for the job, making himself not only dirty and dishevelled but shambling and "down and out". Here he had an astonishing success because he was never challenged by a real tramp or workhouse official. It was an ordeal itself to give up clean cigarettes and depend on finds in the gutter. He slept in monstrously overcrowded casual wards, on one occasion next to a lunatic who spent the night rubbing his sores. He discovered that the Oxford "spike", one of the best in the country, was avoided by tramps because the rules were kept there and one of the most popular was one of the worst, three miles away at Headington where there was no supervision: "the tramps were allowed to crowd at the gates until opening hour whether it rained or snowed or blew a hurricane. From six o'clock they had hunks of bread thrown at them and were driven, clean or dirty, drunk or sober, quiet or noisy, quarrelsome or peaceful into a long hut. Those who fought their way first got wood to lie on. Latecomers and those who were not in the mood to fight had to be content with the stone floor. This dreadful place was a dirt-laden hovel, a combined dormitory and lavatory and it was hard to know where one department commenced and the other ended during the excesses of the night." The guardians in charge of this hell were presided over by an embittered ex-army officer. At another bad workhouse the guardians at their meeting before Frank's arrival had considered two proposals, one to spend a trifle on cleaning the place, the second to convert a barn into a garage for the Master's car; the second was passed and the first thrown out. At Bicester, centre of hunting country, the guardians wanted to get the place closed down because there was little use for it, so Frank was turned away when he arrived on a cold November night, threatened to report to the police, and was let in but punished for his insolence by being kept two nights and given enough work to break even his spirit. At Banbury he was touched to be greeted by a porter who said his trousers weren't thick enough for that weather and to be given a luxurious bath. But further on there was further inhumanity, and he concluded, "They do not desire to be cruel. They have simply lost interest in this unending procession of degraded men who present a problem which they do not understand and for which they have no remedy."

He had a high old time exposing the "workhouse hells" in a Sunday paper and his articles shamed the authorities. Reforms followed. But there had been a personal failure.

Once again he had failed to identify himself with "the lowest". The average tramp was hungry, bug-ridden, scrofulous, bullied, tormented, jeered at and utterly despised. But he failed to agree that he was "the lowest". Indeed he thought of himself as something of a hero because he resisted the conventions of society. He would go on tramping till he died in a ditch, rather than stay in a workhouse and reconcile himself to his fate. "No one", wrote Frank with a sort of wonder, "believes himself to be the lowest, neither the criminal nor the tramp nor, indeed, the leaders of society."

Frank, having cast off the prestige of his class, failed to find what he had been looking for. He had made himself an authority on the vagrancy problem and put it to good account; when Bicester workhouse was closed down, it was turned into the Frank Gray Home for Boys and there, as in his own house, he tried to save the young from the road. But he had not genuinely made himself a leader of "the lowest".

There followed the *Oxford Mail* venture which should have provided a permanent scope and direction. But here again there was disappointment. There was a serious quarrel. He complained that there ought to be another local director—his friend Bradley. He always had friends and associates who seemed incongruous and in this case it was a local business man called H. J. Bradley, who started life as a page in the Oxford Union and had become perhaps the most important business man in the city; he owned the fashionable grocers, Grimbly and Hughes, and the George Restaurant which was cooled by a series of remarkable carpet-like fans and where the richer undergraduates threw bread rolls (if not worse) at each other every Saturday night. To a stranger Mr Bradley appeared the archetype of the Conservative business man but he had supported Frank in the elections and Frank wanted him on the *Oxford Mail* board. He said there had been an undertaking but the newspaper group wanted no more local directors. Possibly they were alarmed by Frank's attitude to their business. At any rate, he was soon at loggerheads with the other directors and no doubt he made violent speeches.

He had to have fresh interests.

I was driving into Oxford with him one day when he waved a hand and said "I suppose you realise this is the gateway to one of the most beautiful cities in the world". I had to confess, looking at the mean houses and shops, that I had temporarily overlooked the fact, but Frank was in no mood for hair-splitting. He announced that the gateway to one of the most beautiful cities in the world ought to be marked in some special way and this meant that he was going to start a "Zoo and Pleasure Gardens". What appeared at first to be a *non sequitur* became easier to appreciate when it transpired that he had managed to get hold of just the site for the zoo. This was followed up by the preparation of a list of local dignitaries who were willing to lend their names to the venture in order to prove that it was no sordid money-making business; and I for my part was responsible for an impassioned appeal to the readers of the *Oxford Mail* to subscribe the price of an elephant called Rosie.

At first the venture seemed fun, and it certainly brought out of the backwoods some of Frank's stranger friends, but before long he was exasperated by the whole thing and it petered out in an atmosphere of petty quarrels. But he was not yet completely disillusioned. He was incapable of refusing an invitation to become President of any local society (except for Morris Dancing which he despised), and they ranged from a "Pleasant Sunday Afternoon" (at one of whose meetings Sir Michael

Sadler dropped all his notes before he began speaking and never managed to get them into the right order) to village flower and horticultural shows. Frank had less than average interest in the quality of fruit and vegetables—his attitude may be judged from the fact that visitors to his garden were informed that it contained "over a hundred varieties", though nobody quite knew what they were—but the old light of battle would come into his eye (a phrase he often used) at the prospect of "stirring up" some rustic event which had never known any greater excitement than bowling for a pig or the record size of a vegetable marrow. His first effort to stir up the annual show at the nearest large village of Kidlington consisted of pony racing which ended in a riot. Next year he had greyhound racing, where I was able to meet his former client, the dog-breeder, Bill Jeffries, still in a cut-away coat and leaning his six feet four inches on a shepherd's crook. Mr Jeffries remained as confident in picking greyhound winners as when he used to run races at hunt meetings; and when he had breezily advocated the claims of animals in four separate races which romped home miles ahead of the field I asked him how he did it, to which he loftily replied: "I ought to know 'em since I've seen 'em all warned off the proper tracks." At the end of the proceedings, some of the punters who had not been in the know assembled round the judge's tent making menacing noises, but Frank was as innocent of greyhound racing as of marrow judging and escaped unscathed.

It was an odd thing that all his ventures ended in a doubtful and equivocal atmosphere: the Parliamentary career, the *Oxford Mail*, the zoo and smaller things. One of the smaller things was his association with me, for it suddenly became clear that he expected more publicity for one of his stunts than I wanted to give, that I was in a difficult position and that I had better leave Shipton. He disapproved, but I went.

Because I saw less of him during the next year or two his bright "puckish", "impish" manner began to seem less convincing when we did meet and I began to feel nervous of some unpredictable catastrophe. I was much involved (perhaps too much) with University affairs at a time when the best known undergraduates lived in a febrile atmosphere of scandal, intrigue and showman-ship, and it was a matter for embarrassment when Frank sent a perfectly serious message to that extraordinary lark the Oxford Balloon Union. When his marriage broke up and the judicial separation was reported he would allow himself no normal emotion but said with an alarming grin: "Well, we're getting plenty of publicity—of a kind we could do without" (a quo-tation from somebody involved in his parliamentary petition). When I went out to Shipton and found that a butler had been installed, I had a sense of artificiality and discomfort. It was intolerable that Frank Gray of all people should be alone in a house, with a butler.

Frank's last quarrel, so far as I know, was with Dr Phelps, Provost of Oriel. Dr Phelps will be remembered for many things, including his black boater and the fact that he used to retire from the Oriel High Table, take a large pinch of snuff and then burst into whinnies of laughter which the under-graduates imitated. At the time he was heavily engaged as Chairman of the Oxford Guardians and Frank questioned his methods at the workhouse.

One day, in 1935, I was telephoned and asked whether I could go out to Shipton immediately. Frank was in bed. His grin looked as if it was painted on his shrunken face and his eyes burned. He was not smoking but he coughed nevertheless. He had had a small advertisement put in several national papers. This advertisement was for "tramp vagrants" who would help in an investigation of the casual wards. Some of the replies were from genuine tramps (they are great newspaper readers, though late) some from tramp-majors, some from unemployed men. Frank wanted me to draft a reply telling them to be in Oxford on a certain day. They were to come to the newspaper office, and there every man would be given half a crown for coming and half a crown for every day he stayed in Oxford. They were to spread the news on the roads and get together as many as possible.

The men would go to the Oxford casual ward, where not a fraction of them would be able to get in (the shortage of accom-modation was apparently Dr Phelps's fault) and then the word was to be spread among them—here Frank became alarmingly conspiratorial—that the colleges were open to all visitors. Men were to be encouraged to go there and "drum up" in the quadrangles. When the reporters (let alone the Fellows) wanted to know what was the meaning of this extraordinary scene, it would all come out that the wretched Dr Phelps had brought this upon Oxford because of his incompetent handling of the Oxford Board of Guardians.

Looking back, I have some regret that I failed to enter into the spirit of this scheme. A few hundred desperate men "drumming up" in Tom Quad or New College gardens might have given the academicals a salutary glimpse of the raw. But shrink I did and, having recovered my breath, worked hard to convince the bed-ridden man that, brilliant though the scheme was, it might misfire without his guiding hand and ought to wait, surely, until he was hale and hearty. He looked disappointed, but eventually assented with his Oxfordshire "Oo-ah".

After some more talk I went down to the silent hall, a stone-flagged room hung with his African trophies. I ought to have stood there and thought of all the scenes that had taken place here when the master was the great showman. But what I believe I felt as I pulled the door open was a cowardly relief that I had managed to get myself out of the position for which he had chosen me—the inciter of the vagrant mob.

He went away to Africa to try to get back his health, but he died on the ship outside Southampton, aged 55. He was taken to Wolvercote cemetery on a fire-engine, followed by two young men, the sons of a friend who were the last people to help him preserve the illusion of youth. The most noticeable people in the cemetery on that cold wet day were women with prams and it seemed unbelievable that there were no bands, no columns of civic representatives, above all no admirers who could have been said to represent the mob.

Two days later, I had a letter from Mrs Gray saying that she had come down from London in the evening, stood at the grave alone and gone back. So ended the Grays in Oxford. They had been here for only 65 years.